What people are saying about

Who is in?

This book, centered around the questions, "Who's in? Who am I?", and "Who's aware of the experience?", came to me at a time when I found myself in a void, with little else to do but to surrender to whatever processing is needed, making these questions more relevant than ever. I thought I could "just read" the book but found myself in tears reading only the first half of the prologue. Taking in one page, even one line at times, the words keep hitting all the spots where I can no longer find anything to hide behind. I read, experience, follow the words with a defenseless heart, with every word falling into place. Sometimes I find myself crying, sometimes laughing, never indifferent, sleepless at times, and always, always drifting into silence, in awe of expanding beyond.

As an Osho sannyasin I'm no stranger to the questions and processes that are being presented, so well laid out, in this book. The clear, razorblade-sharp writing only deepens the experience. And the soul, once addressed and having tasted glimpses of its true nature, only calls louder: I Am, here, now, until "I am" dissolves. It's astonishing how universal, unique, this experience is.

I'm reading: "This life, this planet, this universe feeds not on hope but on PRESENCE.

And Presence is rebellion."

I think of all my compromising, my betrayals of Truth. Will I have the courage to rebel? To live totally? What do I sense when I ask myself these questions?

This book leaves me with a clear set of tools, and the warm and comforting realization that I don't need to *do* anything. *Who is in? Beyond Self-image* certainly reminds me I already embody it.
Caroline Beumer-Peeters, psychotherapist, trainer, author of *Solution Focused Coaching for Adolescents*

Praise for The Author's Other Work

Without a Mask will take you on an exciting journey. It will give you tools to use to discover who it really is behind the mask we all wear... the mask we hide our real selves behind in order to belong and fit in with our families and the society in which we live.

The process the author takes you through is logical and experiential. It is not a process that you will do once but several times. For me it has given me timely reminders of what I already "know" and prompted me to keep using these techniques in my life. For the beginner, you will learn interesting facts on child development and up-to-date research that underpin the information the mystics have always known. The tools the author gives us are easy to implement. I have no hesitation in recommending *Without a Mask* as an aid on your inner journeying. Quoting Costantino, "... an incomparable adventure, a journey of awakening..."

Definitely a "keeper" for me.

Shaz Goodwin, Goodreads.com

Freedom to Be Yourself is a very deep and thorough look into how our own personal judgment can impact on our lives, and perhaps more importantly, who we are.

The book is divided into four parts: Recognizing the Presence of the Inner Judge, Freedom from the Judge, Being Yourself, and Experiences. In these sections we are taken through a variety of subjects including what is the inner judge?, gossip, guilt, sexuality and spirituality. The book is illustrated throughout with case studies, depicting the lessons mentioned in the chapters, and how the issues were dealt with/overcome.

At the end of each chapter, exercises are provided to help you understand and explore the lessons covered. These exercises challenge you to face the truth about who you are, and why you are like the way you are; they make you face what is real in your life. By working through these little exercises, you will come to know yourself better and on a much deeper level.

This book gives us much to think about, especially in terms of who we are, who we appear to be, and how we measure personal worth. I would recommend this to those who wish to gain a deeper understanding of themselves and to those who find themselves asking, "Who am I?"

Sammi Cox, author of *One Turn of the Wheel*

I found Avikal Costantino's book on *Freedom to Be Yourself: Mastering the Inner Judge* inspiring, easy to read and extremely practical. He obviously understands the subject well, and presents it in a way that can lead people to do their own work on overcoming the tyranny of their inner judge. As a seminar leader who deals with this theme, I find this book a great contribution to the work and will not hesitate to recommend it to our participants.

Dr. Krishnananda Trobe, author of *Face to Face with Fear* and *When Sex Becomes Intimate*

Who is in?

Beyond Self-image

Who is in?

Beyond Self-image

Avikal E. Costantino

Winchester, UK
Washington, USA

JOHN HUNT PUBLISHING

First published by O-Books, 2022
O-Books is an imprint of John Hunt Publishing Ltd., 3 East St., Alresford,
Hampshire SO24 9EE, UK
office@jhpbooks.com
www.johnhuntpublishing.com
www.o-books.com

For distributor details and how to order please visit the 'Ordering' section on our website.

ISBN: 978 1 78535 947 7
978 1 78535 948 4 (ebook)
Library of Congress Control Number: 2021952107

A CIP catalogue record for this book is available from the British Library.

Design: Matthew Greenfield

UK: Printed and bound by CPI Group (UK) Ltd, Croydon, CR0 4YY
Printed in North America by CPI GPS partners

We operate a distinctive and ethical publishing philosophy in
all areas of our business, from our global network of authors to
production and worldwide distribution.

Contents

Also by this author

Without a Mask: Discovering Your Authentic Self
978-1-84694-533-5

Freedom to Be Yourself: Mastering the Inner Judge
978-1-78099-191-7

When the Ocean Dissolves into the Drop: Osho, Love, Truth
and me
978-8868953874

Lust, Love and Prayer – Lussuria, Amore e Preghiera
978-8892347410

"Who is in?" is a Koan.

Koan, Japanese (in Chinese gōngàn) – Merriam-Webster: a paradox to be meditated upon that is used to train Zen Buddhist monks to abandon ultimate dependence on reason and to force them into gaining sudden intuitive enlightenment.

This book is dedicated to four magnificent women whose names begin with Prem, the Sanskrit for Love: Prem Kendra, Prem Anando, Prem Ganga and Prem Amira.

Introduction

The search for the fundamental identity of the subject of our existence has been part of the history of humanity for millennia. It has taken various forms and has been embodied in various questions: "Who am I?" "Where am I?" "What is the nature of I?" and, more recently, "Who is in?" introduced by Osho, the Indian mystic; my master, guide and friend.

The Awareness Intensive Retreat is a classic retreat of meditation and self-inquiry in which you contemplate and communicate the experience of total immersion in this question, three or seven days, and sometimes fourteen and twenty-one.

Each retreat is an adventure to the borders of the inner world, beyond the known, beyond conventions, beliefs, the illusions of certainty with which we hold our fragile descriptions of the Real together. When we go inside and really look, inevitably everything we think we know about ourselves and the world we live in begins to dissolve and show itself for what it is: ideas, concepts, stories and self-hypnosis to enable survival.

The question tears through the shadows, lifts veils, dissolves our defence structures, and the Real shines, illuminates, envelops and fills us. The ancient mystical description of The Whole that is revealed is clear, evident and intimate: Truth, Goodness and Beauty.

When we get to the point of asking ourselves questions like "Who is in?", "Who am I?" then there is no return. The inner journey, the spiritual journey, the journey into the mystery of Being takes a turn whose consequences are impossible to imagine. As the mystical Advaita says: your head is inside the tiger's mouth.

Rarely is this question openly asked. We rarely stop and give ourselves permission and support to look inside directly, with curiosity and affection. It is rare for us to open ourselves to the depths of radical intimacy, without boundaries. We don't venture into this unknown and unpredictable being that is each of us. Yet these questions – "Who is in?" "Who am I?" "Who is living this life?" "Who wants to know and understand?" – and so many equally fundamental questions underlie every moment of our lives, whether they are pronounced, or appear as flying birds or ghosts in the misty awareness of sleep. It is our soul and our humanity that inevitably remember them, pray them, meditate them, tell them and throw them into the unknown space of the present moment, and in the interval we are suspended; every moment between life and death. That moment is blessed when we notice them and hear their sound; that moment when we hear the words formulated, when we risk opening up this immense unknown space: "Who is in?"

But why ask ourselves these questions? What are the benefits of openly asking who I am or who is in or other similar questions?

The answer is quite simple: these questions and the resulting exploration open us up to the possibility of experiencing non-ordinary states of consciousness; non-ordinary in the sense that either they happen to us and we pass through them unknowingly, or that we do not even know or think that they are possible.

These states of consciousness are, however, part of humanity and are described in different ways and forms by mystics, poets, artists, spiritual masters, lovers, shamans, saints, musicians, dancers, great athletes, philosophers and scientists, and many others. Each state is characterized by a wider and deeper presence, by a clearer and more immediate meaning, by a natural and effortless dynamism, by an increasingly complete and precise perception, by an increasingly intimate sense of self and world, up to absolute identity. Everything becomes more real. These questions offer us access to the direct experience of truth. Not only the relative experience of which we experience every moment, but also the ultimate truth of Being incarnate, beyond personality and the individual. This is called "Absolute Subjectivity", "Supreme Identity", "Authentic Self", or the "Point of Light".

In this understanding and direct experience of our True Nature the treasures of the Universe, of the Awakened Consciousness, of the divine that manifests itself in the uniqueness of each of us, open up.

In the following chapters you will find more detailed, perhaps familiar, descriptions of the different states of consciousness, which are mentioned here: State of wakefulness, Dream, Deep Sleep, Observer, and finally, the one until now universally recognized as the highest and all-encompassing called "Non-dual Unity" or "Unity Consciousness".

Experiencing these states of consciousness through direct, immediate, authentic and original experience is generally called Awakening, Illumination, Metanoia, Supreme Realization, and is the natural flourishing of the potential of every human being.

In the following chapters you will find the testimony of my direct experience of these states, and how these experiences were the result of years of personal search and continuous practice and dedication to the existential questions, "Who is in?" and "Who am I?"

You'll find examples and understandings, techniques, and invitations to experiment with self-inquiry with more familiar questions. You will find descriptions of particular qualities that manifest themselves and develop through self-exploration and the experience of non-ordinary states of consciousness. You will find reflections on discipline and surrender. You will find dimensions of the human as they are embodied in me and learn that they are at the same time universal gateways to cosmic consciousness, to Being. You will find pieces written from the belly, others from the heart and others from the head, with different languages and atmospheres in a web of interdependency made of understandings, revelations and actions that feed each other and support each other. In some chapters the various pieces are part of a warp and there is an obvious unity; in others this unity is not explicit, and the various pieces appear as independent, sometimes even isolated. You will find contradictions and paradoxes, polarity and conflict. All are forms in awareness and of awareness, intrinsically and inevitably part of and the expression of the One who does not have a two. You will also find opportunities for self-inquiry in many chapters through questions associated with specific aspects of our life experience and search, and the invitation is to dive deeply into these questions either on your own by writing or, much more powerfully, with someone else, giving you each time to explore.

The structure of this book is based on sacred numbers and their interrelations.

There are 63 fragments, organized in 9 groups of 7. The last 3 fragments include no quote.

I have also included 8 sections of 5 minutes each of free communication for a total of 40 minutes, which is the usual length of a communication exercise in the Awareness Intensive Retreats.

Prologue

As I drift into sleep, I wonder what drives me to write what I will write, and what arrives is, "Beauty." There is a beauty within each of us waiting only to be seen, felt, recognized, shared. It is a beauty that I have no words to express directly. I know that it is made of attention and tenderness, innocence and devotion, curiosity, passion and amazement. I also know that it is this beauty that finally frees us from guilt, shame and fear to being authentic and unique. This beauty is in each of us and does not belong to anyone in particular; we all contribute to its splendor. It is a mystery that surrounds me in which I can dream and not know.

Osho left, to me, to all his disciples and to all of humanity his dream before leaving the body, thirty years ago. This dream is clear: Love and Awareness HERE/NOW.

The word dream can be misleading and have us believe this is a project, a vision for the future: it is not.

Instead, it is the ground of practice moment by moment: BEING love and awareness here/now. Not feeling, making, having, giving, receiving love. Not seeking, recognizing, sharing, being aware of love. BEING LOVE AND AWARENESS.

The focus is neither on the other nor on an object. It is not on acting, it is only and completely on the subject, on you and me. The question is simple, direct, understandable: AM I love and awareness now?

It is like a rock thrown into a lake of uncertainty; a lake made of many "I don't knows", some "Yeses" and some "Nos".

This "I don't know", this uncertainty, is blessed because it opens us up to the reality of the here/now that is alive, unknown, unpredictable, mysterious and beautiful. And in this openness, vulnerability, in this presence without choice we can find that it is our nature TO BE LOVE AND AWARENESS.

Thoughts and memories flow throughout the night inside and around my body and soul, floating in the mystery of this and every moment, surrender, submission, delight of being without boundaries or knowledge. The subtle and living joy of now unfolds without meaning, construct, sense...

freedom kind friend
of silence
sacred word
submission
and
delicate beauty.

One

Oh, my God! ... The direct experience!

Satori is like lightning – you can see a glimpse of the whole, all that is there, and then it disappears. But you will not be the same again. It is not final enlightenment, but a great step towards it. Now you know. You have had a glimpse, now you can search for more of it. You have tasted it, now buddhas will become meaningful.
Osho, mystic

The taste of the Real is intoxicating! To glimpse what really exists behind the veil of our illusions, hopes, descriptions, prejudices and concepts is indescribably exciting and frustrating at the same time. It is like tasting Ambrosia and then returning to flat and repetitive everyday fast-food.

And where is it written that it has to be so? Where does it say that just a little taste is all we deserve? This terrible habit of mediocrity, the diminishing of our being, the boxing in of our uniqueness and its potential within the "acceptable" limits with which we continue to hypnotize ourselves and are being hypnotized. Why? What do we gain from making ourselves small and hoping for a brighter future that denies the light of THIS moment?

The Koan "Who is in" has two fundamental tasks: the first is to take us completely and exclusively into the present, here and now; the second is to invite the Direct Experience of our True Nature, the absolute subjectivity of I AM.

Direct Experience simply means that we know every aspect of the Real, including of course ourselves, in a direct and immediate way without filters of any kind: concepts, beliefs, opinions, ideas, points of view and values. We know each aspect beyond time and space. When we have filters in place there is inevitably selection and interpretation, distance and separation: the experience is not direct, it is mediated. In the direct experience the subject and the object disappear, the two become ONE, whole. The daily experiences that come closest to direct experience are orgasm, emotional and physical elation through creativity, contact with nature, deep meditation and moments of mystical enrapture or prayer. Those who have these experiences either disappear as actors and are dissolved in what is, or the whole fills them and erases them.

Direct experience is a moment when all descriptions of the Real collapse together including the collapse of the distinction between inside and outside. These boundaries which actually only exist as thought-forms which are given consistency through compulsive and hypnotic repetition are finally realized to be false. In direct experience the separation between conscious and unconscious dissolves, the division between light and darkness, the boundary between body and spirit all dissolve. An unpredictable and very simple sense of unity of all that is manifests and envelops us.

Direct experience is called Satori in the Zen tradition.

Hear what Osho says about this word…

SATORI has two meanings. One is the SATORI-state in which everybody is: the birds and the trees and the mountains and you and all the Buddhas – past, present and future. The whole existence is in the state of SATORI. This is another way of saying that God is everywhere, in everything; that God is the soul of everything. Buddhahood is everybody's nature. And the second is the SATORI-event. Every man is from all eternity in the state of SATORI. The SATORI-event is only that historic, anecdotal instance when man suddenly recognizes that he has always been in the SATORI-state. You are a Buddha. When you recognize it, or when you remember it, that is the SATORI-event. The SATORI-event is only a window into the SATORI-state, and this SATORI-event has apparent reality only in the eyes of the man who has not yet experienced it. One who has experienced it recognizes that he has always been in SATORI.

The Sun Rises in the Evening, Chapter 1

The most immediate and alive implication of recognizing "I have always been in the state of Satori" is the recognition that there is only direct experience every moment, and that if I do not see it, if I do not feel it, if I do not enjoy it, it is not because it does not exist, but only because I am not present. I am identified with the structure of personality and limitation. I am identified with the veils that hide that Satori-state which is always and already.

The recognition of the Satori-state is not necessarily difficult; what is often difficult is to accept the naked truth that the Satori-state opens up moment by moment. The sometimes-vertical fall of our projections on things and people can be difficult to bear, and the tendency to inertia and returning to conditioned states of consciousness can be very appealing. The old comfort zones are not only familiar but also well tested and easy to embody. Many might find themselves, often for a long time, in a latent schizophrenia between the attachment to the Satori-event and the liberation they tasted, and the familiar, albeit narrow, comfort of personality and its habits.

An inevitable recognition gradually dawns on us: that what we imagined as the end is, on the contrary, the starting point and beginning. As Osho says in one discourse, "We encounter a sign where on one side is written 'Here the world ends' and, when we look at the other side we read, 'Here God begins'."

What does it mean to live God in everyday life? What does it mean to look, feel, move, talk, eat, write, make love, walk from the space of the divine? In the space of the divine? Living expression of the divine incarnate?

A succinct indication by Nisargadatta Maharaj: "Whatever happens, happens to you by you, through you; you are the creator, enjoyer and destroyer of all you perceive." And another one by Ramesh Balsekar: "Understand that nothing happens unless it is God's will and do what you like. What can be simpler than that?"

Every moment, every act, every event IS direct experience. Your eyes are open. Your heart is open to everything without any exclusion. Your mind is pure infinite space, pure awareness in which all forms appear and disappear, without leaving a trace. Actions take place without the doer. Freedom is absolute and unnecessary.

Two seconds of nothingness

And over time that's all I wanted, those two seconds of nothingness.
Rue, in *Euphoria*, S1 E1

1.

Rue is a teenage girl in a television series called *Euphoria*. A teenager who lives on the razor's edge of despair with the need for ecstasy and dissolution, the continuous and methodical compensation of the extreme, and above all drugs of all kinds. She is pushed by that one hope: to be able to re-experience that miraculous silence, that emptiness and that quiet where there are no thoughts, emotions and needs. It is not only teenagers who feel this despair and that need for peace, but all of humanity and it is enough to turn our attention to human history to simply recognize that it is the search for those two seconds of nothing in our craving for sex, alcohol, drugs, meditation, religion, wars, gambling, workaholism, addiction to danger, prayer, politics, money. Everything in our collective history speaks of the desire to be able to say one day, "At last, I am at home and there is nothing more to do, to try, to prove, to achieve; I can stop and be at peace with myself and the world."

The fundamental difference between adolescents and so-called adults is that the adolescents are generally not yet completely desensitized, anesthetized by years of complete identification with things, with objects, with doing and complete forgetfulness of themselves. In them the wound of betrayal of their true nature is still fresh, still incomprehensible, still on the surface and the pain is alive. They are still close, and perhaps even remembering their innocence. Those two seconds of nothing where the noise of the mind, the images of our personal history, the memories of our wounds and triumphs, successes and failures, where the voice of the inner judge, everything disappears and only I AM remains.

2.

Spiritual search is in most cases confused groping, with highs that we tend to grasp and lows that we try to escape, which persecute us due to our attachment to personality and the need for certainty. Spiritual search seeks reasons, meaning, explanations, inspiration, escape from mediocrity and the daily grind, and is in many ways not much different or more effective than any drug, shopping, the illusions of specialness that the world offers us continuously through a thousand traps. Spiritual search can, like anything else, be a diversion, a compensation, a way to avoid emptiness and lack; an idealized groping towards those two seconds of nothingness. Any search, even if we do not label it with the adjective "spiritual", arises from a need: to know, to possess, to understand, to balance things, to find ourselves, to justify, to give meaning and so on. Behind the need there is often a sense of lack, perhaps unclear, perhaps unidentified, but somehow felt; an emptiness that is often familiar to us and that we generally tend to avoid or hide from ourselves, until, either by chance or out of desperation, we find ourselves looking. Sometimes there is also just the opposite: the sudden, unexpected appearance of something different, completely different from what we are used to. Something that resonates in deep and forgotten parts of us, like those two seconds of nothingness that in their nothingness are full and resonant with peace and freedom.

3.

We don't take drugs because we are social misfits who lack contact. We don't gamble because we have few morals. We are not looking for sex or power because we are compulsively in need of recognition and discharge. We do not abuse ourselves with excess work or alcohol or throw ourselves into prayer or meditation or sport to escape a dehumanizing reality. Of course, this is there, but the fundamental thrust is: I want to be myself. It is a natural and inevitable drive towards the realization of our uniqueness. An evolutionary need to manifest in a concrete way why we are here, each of us, whatever it costs. This search sometimes opens the door for an understanding of absolute importance: the recognition that I miss something and that feeling this lack terrifies me. This is what I call the "negative emptiness" experience.

Generally, the door closes, or we close it, with extreme speed because this vacuum can be paralyzing and is generally associated with an immediate sense of danger and indescribable pain. It is as if all the monsters of our childhood, all the most terrifying memories, begin to agitate as deep currents in our psyche threatening to submerge us. The search is not a choice; it is a primordial need for survival of our soul. It is an absolutely illogical and irrational intuition that the terrifying void is the door to resurrection. In that knowing, investigating, surrendering to nothingness, to that void, I can be reborn like the phoenix. And that's exactly how it is.

4.

When I was little the void did not frighten me; I remember it. I remember it because I remember very clearly how much all the adults around me did their best to get me out of that void. On the other hand, what choice did my parents, relatives, teachers really have when one of the classic sayings of our culture is: An empty mind is the devil's workshop. Being empty is diabolical! Yet, it is enough to notice with attention and affection the small child to see how his emptiness is only the other side of his fullness, how his vital totality manifests itself naturally and efficiently through a complete process of energetic charge and discharge. When fullness is expressed there is complete discharge and in the void that manifests itself there is life that fills that organism open to receive and recharge. Loading and unloading, loading and unloading, full and empty, full and empty. And then, little by little, they teach us mediocrity, through the fear of being too much and/or too little. We forget what it's like to be totally full, and fulfilled, and totally empty, and fulfilled. The opposite of mediocrity is not excellence, it is totality. Being oneself totally, unequivocally, totally full and totally empty, and everything in between.

Rebellion and revolution

The rebel simply says goodbye to the past.
Osho

They taught us to hope by shifting our attention and our ability to "see" away from the present, from the here/now, to the future.

They taught us that hope is a virtue that will bring us closer to the kingdom of God, to love, to success, to wealth, to our dreams.

They taught us to strive to create a better tomorrow by forgetting this moment and hating all those who strive in ways other than our own way without realizing that we are ALL slaves to an absolute lie.

They have taught us to strive to change things or to preserve them, and in this commitment we have forgotten our humanity which exists in this moment, in the present we share, in the interdependence that unites us, in the evolution, the inevitable sap of existence that EVERYTHING includes.

Revolution is the desire to change things, it is all projected out of itself on objects, be they societies, cultures, religions, ideas, beliefs. Revolution wants to change a status quo to another status quo. An ideology with another ideology. A dominion with another dominion. A purpose with another purpose. Revolution is rarely rebellious, or when it is, it is only for a period of time until it conquers power.

Rebellion can only be in the present, rooted in the here/now, continually subversive with respect to any status quo because rebellion is incarnate truth, and the truth is always new, fresh, unpredictable, unlimited and inclusive. Rebellion is always inherently revolutionary, but it is not against something that it deems wrong or an enemy: rebellion does not judge and exclude; rebellion includes and transcends because Being is ALL there is.

Let us look inside and ask ourselves whether we have the courage and the yearning to be rebellious and discover our uniqueness, to honor it together with that of everyone else. If we are willing to stop hoping and start living this moment with all the truth that it contains. If we are willing to let ourselves be taken by the whirlpools and fireworks of creativity freed from hope, from a "better" tomorrow, from "one day when..."

This life, this planet, this universe feeds not on hope but on PRESENCE.

And Presence is rebellion.

That magical place...

I want to take you to a place of pure magic... It's the place athletes call the "zone". Buddhists call "satori" and ravers call "trance".

I call it the Silver Desert. It's a place of pure light that holds the dark within it. It's a place of pure rhythm.
Gabrielle Roth

More and more frequently I am asked what meditation is and if I meditate. The first question is simple, and I usually answer indicating that there is a substantial difference between meditation techniques and meditation itself. Techniques are ways/processes to learn to practice presence by embodying it, while meditation is the state of pure presence beyond any technique. So, techniques are part of the world of form and are put into action by personality, while meditation is the natural state of Being, a manifestation of its true nature that is Pure Presence and, as Osho speaks of it, it is expressed as Choiceless Awareness.

The second question is more complex because it implies a paradoxical answer: *It is I who sits down, it is not me who is sitting.*

Let me explain: for many years I have been waking up in the middle of the night, usually between one and three o'clock. I get up. I go to sit and meditate. I don't use a particular technique. I don't do Vipassana or Zazen. I don't focus on anything specific; I just close my eyes and I'm there. I don't grasp anything, and I don't reject anything: what's there is what's there. My attention is free. I don't have a goal or a set time, I'm sitting for half an hour, an hour, or more. I know when I'm going to sit down, and I don't know when I'm going to get up. At some point I realize that my eyes open, my body stretches, and I go back to bed. It is I who choose to get out of bed and sit down when I wake up in the darkness. As soon as I close my eyes the sense of me begins to dissolve and there is a clear internal movement where attention shifts from being focused on objects of various types, physical or not, sensations, emotions, thoughts, images, memories, etc., to the space, to the container of objects I experience. This happens on its own.

In this movement various things identifiable at the beginning take place: the boundaries of the body expand and gradually tend to disappear; the perception of time changes radically until I experience "being beyond time"; every object that appears in consciousness is at the same time clearer, more precise, and also immersed in the vastness of the space in which it appears, not separated from it; paradoxically I feel light, evanescent, and completely rooted and centered even if there is no definable center; sometimes slowly, sometimes suddenly, everything dissolves... I could add many other elements, but each description belongs to language, and the truth is that there are no words that can really describe presence. There are no concepts that can depict it, and, above all, there is no entity separated from the presence that experiences it. I'm not there. There is no separation and fundamental subject/object duality. There is no me who is sitting.

When I get up the self comes back, as they say, happy and satisfied.

The technique

Going back to meditation techniques, I know, I've had the experience and I hear it repeated over and over again: sometimes they're boring, repetitive, "I have to make an effort," "I feel like I'm not getting anywhere," "How many years do I have to do them?" Etcetera...

The point of techniques is not to take us to awakening.

How could it be possible that a technique practiced by personality and decided by the conventional self could create spiritual awakening?

The task of the techniques is to frustrate us, to make us thirsty, to keep us on the razor's edge and to push us to ask ourselves continuously: Why do I meditate? What am I looking for? And most importantly, DO I REALLY WANT TO WAKE UP? IS SPIRITUAL AWAKENING THE FIRST AND FUNDAMENTAL ITEM ON MY EXISTENTIAL SHOPPING LIST?

Each technique helps to continuously verify our commitment

to support ourselves in the search; to rekindle our curiosity towards the unknown, our intention to be present with what is, our openness and submission to the Absolute.

Every good technique forces us to ask continuously: WHERE AM I RIGHT NOW? And when we begin to answer with absolute certainty: I am here, then in that solid grounding in the present moment, the mystery of "Who is in?" reveals itself.

Preconceptions

Often when I speak with people it turns out that most people tend to see meditation fundamentally as a state of motionless pacification. For sure, this is one of the qualities through which the Absolute manifests, and... there's so much more!

For example, when the boundaries begin to dissolve and with them possibly even our attachment to particular forms/ objects, an incredible dynamism between space and forms becomes evident. A dynamism that when we immerse ourselves in it shows us the continuous intersection, interdependence, synchronicity of emptiness and fullness, what Buddha pointed at when he said: "Emptiness is fullness, and fullness is emptiness."

In this interdependence we can relax and let the deep currents of the Absolute open the doors of creativity: EROS, the divine spark.

In this synchronicity the richness of the present moment explodes through the myriad of possibilities that turn out as a gift of the Mystery.

Here the dissolution of the conventional self implies awakening to the reality of the co-creation of the present moment. Meditation is LIFE!

Here, another phrase of the Buddha: "Samsara is Nirvana and Nirvana is Samsara", finds roots and realization thus radically upsetting all materialistic and spiritualistic conceptions of the real, and inexorably focusing our attention on the reality of every moment, and the absolute non-separation between everyday life and enlightenment.

Here we can understand that there is a real possibility of meditating not FOR enlightenment but FROM enlightenment, creatively as an expression of your, my, our uniqueness.

As far as I am concerned, I have no doubt that meditation is effective. Effective in opening the door to the direct experience of states of consciousness that go far beyond our usual awareness. It is also clear to me that meditation is absolutely not synonymous with sitting silently in some more or less strange position contemplating one's navel and waiting for visions, angels, liberation, buddhas of various kinds or any special state. Indeed, all this slows down or even prevents the real experience of meditation as pure presence. All of us, in different ways, and almost always unrecognized, find ourselves going through moments, life situations in which we are in meditation even if unknowingly: walking in nature, listening raptured to a piece of music, dancing letting ourselves be possessed by the movement, in intense moments of combat in martial arts, while painting or singing or playing, while we run, swim or surf... The state of flow, where I am one with the environment in which I interact, is meditation! Feeling fully involved in this moment, in this feeling, in this action where there is no separation or distance, this is meditation! Meditation in the world of form and relativity.

And it is essential to recognize it as such to avoid both idealizing meditation by making it something disembodied and almost inhuman, and also to recognize in ourselves a natural capacity intrinsic to our deep nature which acts even when we do not realize it.

Preferences

A question that naturally arises is that if it can be almost easy to flow with "pleasant" things, is it much more difficult, if not impossible, to flow with the "unpleasant" ones?

I think it is clear that the terms "pleasant" and "unpleasant" are relative, to the person, to the situation, to the event, to the state in which we find ourselves, to the need we feel, etc. Things that are unpleasant under certain conditions are easy to deal with if we have a strong motivation or if the conditions (even mental) which implied that judgment change. For example, putting yourself in a dangerous situation can sometimes be pleasant, feeling pain can sometimes get us into expanded states of consciousness. Empathy with the suffering of others can create a state of fusion both inside and outside; if I am hungry, I can ingest and even enjoy food that until recently I would have avoided, and so on.

In many mystical traditions a highly touted technique has to do with acceptance. I'm not a fan of this technique, quite the contrary. I will not go into the deeper implications, but I merely observe that it is a temporary technique that can help to peel our densest layers of resistance and rejection of reality, but that in the long term it implies a constant attention to the objects that we reject. It is ineffective and fundamentally lacking. In addition, especially in countries with a strong Christian tradition, it often coincides with a victimistic and fatalistic ideology: I have to accept, I carry my cross, it is my burden... Much more efficient is to get out of the pleasant/unpleasant dualism by recognizing that it is a mental mechanism, based on cultural, religious, social conditioning (in addition to being one of the fundamental fuels of narcissism), and to radically free ourselves from the mechanism that operates unknowingly creating this division.

For starters, it's about doing something very simple: recognizing that reality is indifferent to whether we accept it or reject it, WHAT IT IS, IS WHAT IS, EVERY MOMENT. So instead of having our attention on the object, event, situation and judgments we have about it, our attention shifts to ourselves, to that "I" who is experiencing: I open all my senses, and I am PRESENT in the recognition of what is there, whatever it is. Practicing CHOICELESS AWARENESS. And I emphasize the word practicing because it is not enough to understand intellectually, it is necessary that we notice as often as possible how we divide reality between good and evil, pleasant and unpleasant, beautiful and ugly, and how we continually cling to our preferences, which are being dictated by the past, and how this prevents us:

a. to perceive directly the present moment;
b. to respond creatively to what is present and therefore destroy EROS, the divine spark of the new that is present at all times;
c. to grow in our ability to include new aspects of the real and new possibilities.

This means using meditation to become aware of resistance and preferences.

And look, I'm not saying that you have to change them, fight them, manipulate them. What I am saying is that by practicing presence with what is, dualism tends to dissolve, boundaries to melt, and we discover the fundamental unity and interdependence at the core of the Great Ground of Being.

Flow is a manifestation of an inner state of non-separation and is independent from the content of the experience.

On acceptance and realization

At any moment I prefer the hard truth to a gentle lie.
True Detective, S3 E8

Spiritual teachers are, for the most part, wonderful scoundrels who, unscrupulously, throw the carrot of acceptance at those who yearn for a life without suffering. So, to entice them to search and invite them to understand a universe much larger than the one in which they live, they show them how their suffering has a lot to do with resistance to life and rejection of parts of themselves and the Real. "Accept. Accept without conditions," they say. They are rascals!

Since the resistances and rejections are often quite evident, new seekers begin to observe their mechanisms and patterns so that they stop themselves resisting, and strive to accept. I stress the word "strive" because, unfortunately, this is the fundamental trap into which almost everyone falls.

Acceptance inevitably implies doing, that there is someone who has the power to accept or not. It implies that the power to change reality is in our hands; the power to change reality as we please, accepting it, rejecting it, hoping for it to be different, condemning it, manipulating it. This goes on and on, and we delude ourselves.

Now the big reveal! The secret of Pulcinella: "reality" does not exist, what does exist is everything that is. When we project on to everything that is our thoughts, emotions, beliefs and expectations then we create what we call "reality". That "reality" is only a description which corresponds to our set of projections, and since we identify with it, it becomes OUR reality.

The dreamer believes he is the dream and in the dream. This process of hypnotic creation is Maya, the illusion of reality.

Remembering the dreamer is the first step to becoming free, the disappearance of dream and dreamer the last. When we recognize that we live in a description, the dream breaks down and the question of acceptance disappears completely replaced by REALIZATION, and that is the simple and immediate recognition of everything that is exactly as it is, without the obscuration produced by our projections, expectations, ideas, prejudices, beliefs, etc. Indeed, to be precise, including all this without limiting ourselves to it. This is what Buddha calls

SUCHNESS.

In realization, the universe in which we live becomes vast, absolutely overflowing with abundance, unpredictable and mysterious, and what we have for years called "reality" is revealed for what it is: a very limited and often repetitive interpretation we have unnecessarily chained ourselves to in order to survive.

It is at this point that we have the opportunity to let go of the daily effort to create a hypothetical certainty associated with a false reality, and we are able to learn to live in uncertainty, which is the true nature of existence.

And when we get to this realization then the masters smile slyly.

Five minutes (1)

I ask myself the Koan: "Who is in?"

I look at the clock on the desktop to know the time I start. As I write, I wonder, "Will what I am writing be interesting?" A smile arrives, followed by a long and deep breath, and I notice a letting go inside in the familiarity of this moment. I write and the Koan resonates inside. It is precise and simple. I'm going to stop. A car passes. The engine noise arrives, then passes. Birds. There is a slowdown. Across my face the sensation of transparency, the gaze blurs and everything widens. Everything? All? I don't know what that means. What widens is the depth of the breath and the space around and inside. Then a new breath arrives, aware of garbage bin noise, lid raising, then dropping. My wrists are resting on the table. Wait, curiosity? I don't know what, perhaps the next breath? There's a sense of lightheartedness and a feeling of lostness and of centeredness simultaneously. A thought recognizes the paradox inherent in this and, possibly, every moment. There was a short break in the fingers before that "possibly"... I cannot say for sure. Thought: "Can I say anything for sure?" I am enjoying writing freely and

I remember how Osho recommended this technique. I don't have a partner to share with. I am my own partner, usually the mirror, now this keyboard. I look at the clock... and I realize that I have forgotten the beginning time... Break... Break... crows outside, noise and other birds. A thought, "I don't know the name." Who is in?... Break... silence inside... and slowing down...

Inquiry (1)

1. Explore your ideas, beliefs, and opinions about the relationship between love and awareness. In particular explore how what you communicate is related to the conditioning you received. When this first picture is clear, close your eyes and bring different experiences to awareness from the ones you described. Experiences that you may not have been able to rationalize, box, compartmentalize into definitions that make sense. Feel in the body what's going on. Feel what's going on energetically, is there expansion or contraction? Do you feel more or less spacious? Avoid judging what comes to you, changing it, controlling it or manipulating it.

2. Explore your relationship with the status quo of personality – how should you be? – explore your availability, capacity, and willingness to question that status quo and the boundaries it implies. In everyday life, are you willing to take a risk? Are you willing to challenge boundaries and limits, or do you tend to adapt and stay in your comfort zone? What are the most obvious effects of how you function? Are you satisfied with your ability to be honest, real, yourself? Explore with kindness and compassion and do not fall victim to your inner judge.

3. Assuming you have some experience with meditation techniques, explore your relationship with meditation.

Why do you meditate? Is there anything you're looking for or wanting to avoid? How do the techniques you use affect your everyday life? What associations, ideas, beliefs, assumptions, prejudices do you have with respect to meditation? What do you expect?

4. Flow: what images, sensations, memories, associations come when you tell yourself this word? Close your eyes for a few seconds and listen, look inside, bring to awareness moments when you felt yourself flowing. What did those moments mean to you?

5. When you look at your life and yourself, where do you recognize strong resistance? In which aspects of your daily life? For example: in relation to your body, in sexuality, in creativity, in relating, in love, in relation to work, money, etc. Without haste, gradually and incrementally explore different areas of life, and notice if and where there is resistance. How does that manifest physically, emotionally and mentally? Notice what kinds of tension come into the body as you explore.

6. Acceptance: what happens to you when you read this word?

7. Have you ever considered the question of identity? What do you need to have an identity for? What happens to you when I ask you to explore these questions? What kind of reactions are triggered? What does your mind tell you, and what sensations do you have in your body? Write everything that comes to mind when you try to define your identity quickly for a few minutes. Write freely and uncensored.

Two

The myth of identity

Be realistic, try the impossible.
Ernesto Che Guevara, revolutionary

Osho and many other spiritual masters insist on saying things that sound absurd like "be nobody", "you're the obstacle" and "get out of the way" – and many more of similar tone. These statements are directly addressing our relationship and understanding of ego and identity.

One of the milestones of quantum physics is the discovery that the relative identity of an object (as shown to a subject) varies depending on the observer. An electron sometimes appears to the observer as a particle sometimes appears as a wave. Similarly, when we observe and are observed, we appear a certain way to an observer, and in other ways to different observers and vice versa. These ways change all the time as the observer changes.

So firstly, the identity you carry, and of which you might be proud, serves little or no use. The stability that it seems to give us is just an idea. This identity that we believe to be us is the central point of a set of images of ourselves that have been created over time in relation to external objects (parents first, people, things, situations, events, etc.). Perhaps this is what makes it so difficult for many people to investigate their inner images. They believe that their identity depends on those images of themselves they carry with them, and so they believe that if they question the images, or even let them go, a potential monster will come out thus presenting the question, "WHO AM I?"

As this question arises, the identity we built on the foundations of those images completely shatters. And I say "completely" because the identity of most people is something vague and fragmented already, whether they are consciously aware of this or not.

So, this may prompt you to ask, "How can I live without an identity?"

When you think about it, we already live without identity most of the time. You don't need to know who you are, or to have an idea of who you are to climb the stairs, to read, to cook, to make love, to drive a car, to play, to hammer a nail, or write a blog, and for thousands of other everyday occurrences. You do not need your identity to feel your emotions, to feel what's happening in your body, or to be aware, for example, right now as you read. Identity is something that in everyday occurrence is mostly unnecessary, indeed sometimes it is a real impediment. So, what do we need identity for? It is of no use other than to enclose ourselves within a description made up of the accumulated past. It is a utilitarian issue, providing others with a reference to us, and us to them. We need a name so others can call us and refer to us. We need an identity so we can refer to ourselves and the accumulation of experiences that correspond to that identity as defined by certain parameters and interpretations (personal history); for example, we need it to fill in various forms for work, doctor, borders, school, etc. We also need it to place ourselves within various hierarchies, family, school, work, religious, national, etc.

Identity is a social contract not an existential reality: I AM (without definitions of any kind) is an existential and direct experience (not mediated by acquired knowledge), and we recognize it because we experience it moment by moment, moment after moment. We do not need a name to feel that we exist. We do not need an identity card to feel that we breathe, or that we are excited. We do not need to attach ourselves to a definition to feel that we are here now. Let us stop believing in the fiction of an identity and begin to know ourselves in our integrity and humanity.

This is self-remembering and rebellion against the identity contract.

Reflections on emptiness

And you will know that you have never slept, that you have never dreamed, that you have never been limited to any thing that has appeared, you have never been in any condition you have assumed. There was always only Reality Itself, your True Nature, which is Love-Bliss, Consciousness, the Unqualified Intensity.
Adi Da Samraj, mystic

1.

1. "I miss him so much" – negative emptiness
2. "I don't know which way to turn anymore" – space opens up
3. "I don't know" – creative space
4. "Nothing is missing" – emptiness of objects
5. "I am here" – void full of presence
6. "I am all there is" – emptiness is fullness, fullness is emptiness... Buddha knew it well...

Exploring the Koans "Who is in?" and "Who am I?" is an effective way to experience emptiness. Inquiry into these existential Koans opens two fundamental dimensions of the void. The first is the "emptiness of objects" through the realization that we are not the objects that appear in awareness, be they material or immaterial. The second dimension they open is the collapse of our identification with body, mind and emotions. When the attention finally turns to the subject, not only does the disappearance of the same occur (no objects, no subject) but it is also understood, experientially, that the subject is empty, and this is referred to as the "emptiness of self". The first –

emptiness of objects – frees us from the limiting constraint of factors not intrinsic to our nature (conditioning); the second – emptiness of self – also frees us from identification with false identity revealing it for what it is, a collection of images and memories in time and space accumulated over many years.

2.

An important part of spiritual search has to do with the creation of a supporting environment aligned with our true nature and responding to our need for authenticity and freedom. Just as we learn to sustain ourselves by practicing presence and inquiry, recognizing the emptiness of objects (freedom from conditioning) and the emptiness of self (freedom from egoic identity), so we then learn to "support the void", and we do this explicitly, through the questions, "Who is in?" and "Who am I?" Or implicitly, through the question, "Who is aware of the experience?"

Explicit means that WE DIRECTLY focus our attention on the belief that we exist as a separate self, identified with and through the objects of experience.

Implicit means that our attention, although present in the objects of experience, also focuses on the undeniable presence of the awareness that we are, at the center of every experience. This second question, "Who is aware of the experience?" opens up the recognition of the paradox of the "I" as presence/absence. "I" does not exist as a separate identifiable and personal entity and, at the same time, impersonal awareness is embodied in a personal way that is "I". For example, it is "I" who is aware of all objects; being and not-being are inextricably present and synchronic at any point.

Thus, supporting emptiness means knowingly supporting the paradox of emptiness that is full of presence.

When I support myself, I do not stop at acknowledging the support I give myself in the form, I also recognize that there is no self who supports anyone.

Emptiness supports fullness, and fullness supports emptiness. Freedom is complete and inclusive. It does not reject anything, and it chooses nothing.

3.

When you forget that you are the subject and you identify with the objects of the experience... THIS IS THE ORIGINAL SIN, THE FORGETFULNESS OF YOUR TRUE NATURE, "getting lost in things...", "the fall from heaven", "being enchanted by the sirens". Here is the source of the deepest and most intimate pain, the daily betrayal of who you are ALWAYS and ALREADY.

Castrated and idealized religiosity has proposed to us for millennia renunciation of objects, of pleasure, of the world, of... oh my god "temptations!!!"

Do like Ulysses, do not give up hearing the siren singing, instead find a master tree where you can bind yourself and find support, do not run away, do know directly! This main tree is already in each of us. It is the Essential Will, the solid mountain, the clear intention that sustains us on the journey and allows us to consciously taste everything; ambrosia and poison. Spirit is THE ONLY reality, how can it hurt us?

This column of presence exists in the body and goes from our genitals to the top of our heads. It is in our spine, in its vitality and in its ability to consciously connect Gravity and Grace. When we remember, when we return to the subject, when we make that 180 degree turn and turn our attention from outside to inside then we are able to begin to notice that the awareness of "I am" does not require effort or project, time or direction. You are already aware of the words you read, of the eyes following the lines, of the air you breathe and of the light. There is no need to search. There is nothing to achieve or conquer. This awareness is already here, it is ALWAYS here, and YOU ARE THAT.

4.

The central pointer of meditation is – awareness without choice embodied in "Be still and know". The experience of not choosing an object as it manifests in consciousness – not grasping or rejecting – reveals the VOID, the void in which everything appears and disappears. In this experience I have no preferences, I do not choose, I only reflect every object that emerges exactly as it is without attaching value, meaning, like/dislike to it. No "I want it", "I do not want it". I rest motionless in awareness without choice... I AM STILL, PURE AWARENESS WITHOUT CHOICE. I am also the subject, the specific form through which this awareness, this primary consciousness, manifests itself, the eternal I AM.

In this experience, pure subjectivity, the I AM, can SEE the previous moment, just passed, just before now, and the previous subject that has incarnated becoming an object: I AM THIS, I AM THAT. It is the perennial movement of creation/evolution where the subject continuously becomes the object of the new subject. AND YOU, THE UNIQUE FORM THAT SPIRIT TAKES MOMENT AFTER MOMENT, ARE THE VEHICLE OF THIS CREATION/EVOLUTION. Eros is the spark of this creation/evolution.

5.

And now we come to the question of SPIRITUAL AWAKENING, which means "of Spirit", "to Spirit" and "in Spirit".

Something is radically changing in the world. All the notions of awakening as something absolutely individual need to be reviewed and possibly abandoned. Along with abandoning those notions we also need to let go of the idea that awakening is an event of liberation and cataclysmic final realization. This idea has never reflected reality, but rather was the projection of an idealization and childish desire of seekers. In the age of communication and daily scientific discoveries the dynamics of awakening are also changing and have multiple presentations; consider these:

Aligning with what is the natural experience of the daily awakening of the body, so the awakening of the soul is increasingly recognized as a process, a succession of "ah" moments, which manifest as a more stable and continuous contact with "Spirit in Action".

It is more and more apparent that the awakening of the individual does not take place in isolation but within and as an effect of their relation to the world (no cave, no renunciation).

Awakening sometimes occurs collectively in the congregation of conscious individuals as collective consciousness making a quantum leap beyond the sum of individual consciences.

Awakening begins to present itself as an irregular and unpredictable succession of collapses and regroupings of personality structures within the emergence of Spirit revealing and illuminating reality through the "Void of objects" and the "Void of self".

The Cup of Buddha

Hell is truth seen too late.
Thomas Hobbes, philosopher

Before Buddhism became, like many other religions, an institution, and its monks, priests, ministers, etc. began to live on the shoulders of their faithful, Buddha disciples followed some simple precepts:

They moved every two or three days from one place to a new one. This gave them opportunities to meet new people and new realities all the time, thus tasting the immense diversity we live in and the impermanence of every aspect of life.

They were also continually driven to observe their attachment to external situations and to let go of it. Being human this attachment sooner or later manifested itself in them.

To eat they asked the people they met to put something in their cup and at the end of the day they ate what they had received.

The cup was much more than a container. It was a daily remembrance of an inner state of total trust and acceptance towards life that always, according to the teachings of the Buddha, "gives us what we need".

I remind you that Buddha's first three or four hundred disciples were emperors, queens, princes, generals, rich merchants, great philosophers, famous courtesans and poets. These were people who knew and had experienced power, wealth and pleasure deeply, and who recognized that no external satisfaction was enough to quench their thirst. They knew that being human was so much more than having and owning things. They knew that without the absolute willingness to recognize the intrinsic abundance of existence there is no living but only surviving regardless of whether the survival is encased in gold, worshipped and envied.

In recent months we have had to deal more than ever with our attachments. The COVID-19 virus has forced us to recognize our concepts and beliefs, our dependence and attachment to what we call freedom of movement. It has brought new awareness to our attachment to the physicality of contact, to shop windows, to money, success, relationships as we know them, our car, and more.

Fundamentally we are obliged to come to terms with our desperate need to cover the reality of existence as absolute unpredictable uncertainty with all the things mentioned above and more.

I want to remind you a line from the *Song of Bacchus*, by Lorenzo the Magnificent:

Be happy if you want to,
For tomorrow may not come.

Centering, what are we talking about?

It's how I learned that the real world doesn't always adhere to logic.
Sometimes down is up, sometimes up is down. Sometimes when you're lost, you're found.
Michael Burnham, *Star Trek: Discovery*

In many spiritual traditions, mystical schools, martial arts, healing techniques, even in modern coaching schools we meet the concept and countless techniques for "centering".

One of the most precise and suggestive images that address this topic is the one used by Buddha when using the term "Dukkha". This word has been translated for centuries as "suffering" and makes some sense because suffering is the result of Dukkha; its effect.

The image that Dukkha represents is much more precise though, more concrete, efficient and above all offers many more understandings and possibilities than the very generic term "suffering". Dukkha represents the state of a wheel whose axis is out of center.

Try to visualize this wheel moving on the ground with its center out of place. Inevitably it moves in an uncertain, uncoordinated way, wobbling, straying. This is Dukkha, and this is, according to Buddha, the usual state of humanity.

The effect of forgetting one's true nature, identifying with false ego identity and functioning through the personality mask is Dukkha.

We move in our lives without a center, without a central point of reference, and the effect of all this is fragmentation, a lack of totality, dissatisfaction and the continuous effort to stand, not stray.

The first understanding from the image that Buddha uses is that to function naturally, to give us the opportunity to directly know our true nature and manifest our uniqueness, an inevitable step is for us to return to the center. But what does this mean and how do you do it?

When personality approaches this concept, "returning to live and function from its center", it inevitably does so from the perspective it knows which is the separation/distinction between center and periphery. This has been my personal experience and the experience of most of the people I have worked with. The personality does this from its dualistic vision of reality, so it continues to look for a "center" thinking, hoping, to move away from the phenomena and events that characterize living on the periphery of personality. These phenomena and events include attachments, relationships, emotionality, compulsive thinking, reactivity and problems; the waves and currents that agitate the sea. When personality approaches centering from this attempt to be centered and "not involved" in the chaos of everyday life it is mostly frustrated and can only be so because it unconsciously keeps nourishing and feeding on the fundamental illusion of separation. Moreover, it constantly reinforces a static, I would say Euclidean and mechanistic view of reality, where straight lines exist and time is something that comes and goes, where mathematics is an absolute certainty, and the results are predictable and controllable. In short, the desire for centering essentially conceals a desire for certainty, stability and control.

In this inner state of duality and separation, the subject continually tries to move away from the periphery, which they believe is the cause of their suffering, and return to the center, possibly "forever". Thus, unconsciously reaffirming and reinforcing with this movement their being out of center as well as the belief that there are two separate realities. One reality made of periphery and "superficiality" and the other of center and "depth". The seeker also convinces themselves that identifying with the periphery is mundane while identifying with the center is spiritual, reproducing once again the separation between sacred and profane.

So, the desire for centering directs our attention, if we are alert, towards an unconscious habit of reinforcing separation and exclusion. And that's great! We can notice our preferences: spiritual, mental, emotional and how we would like to attach to a still and final point "forever"! "Ah, if I was centered, I wouldn't get angry!", "I wouldn't suffer because others don't understand me!", "I wouldn't need to be seen!", "I wouldn't get lost in my emotionality", etc. (Here it would certainly help if you took a moment to investigate what your expectations/ dreams are relating to being centered.)

I am stating here that one of the fundamental results of looking for one's center is to begin to notice what happens in the continuous swing between the periphery and the center (or as we often say: getting lost and finding ourselves), and how the focus can gradually shift from the goal: "I want to be centered, not get lost"... to the recognition of the journey: "I am centering, I am getting lost". As we "notice" we begin to become familiar with – and progressively the clarity emerges that there is – a "subject" who has the experience of being identified with the periphery and the various internal and external phenomena. This is a subject who perceives, thinks, has feelings and sensations, sees, recognizes, evaluates, rejects, welcomes, controls, asks, understands. In short, someone who is aware of, in different ways and gradations, what happens to them moment by moment. Thus, we become aware of a central identity we're used to calling "I".

One day one of his students asked Ueshiba Sensei, the founder of Aikido (a martial art whose name means The Way of Harmony), how he always stayed in the center. He chuckled and replied that they were wrong. To them who continually moved from their subjectivity and identified with the various objects inside and out, ideas, sensations, people, events in a continuous getting lost and finding themselves, it appeared that he was always centered because he was relaxed, present, solid, resilient, capable, open and available, not reactive. The reality – he explained – was different: he moved between center and periphery, subjectivity and objects, at such speed that he appeared absolutely centered; the movement of his attention was so spontaneous and fluid that it dissolved the separation and boundaries between inside and outside, periphery and center, subject and object.

The image used by Buddha hides another brilliant and more fundamental understanding which is that...

The recognition that human suffering is caused by a dysfunction produced by the lack of contact with the subject, the center of every experience, and how this recognition is the necessary step to begin a process of de-identification from the objects in which we continually get lost.

At this point the central question of identity opens. Who is this subject, this self that experiences everything and is aware of everything? (Even when we forget.)

Here the image of the wheel shows the genius of the Master because there is an essential condition for the wheel to work harmoniously when its center has returned to its place, and this condition is that THE CENTER IS EMPTY.

This means that it is not enough to understand that the lack of center and compulsive identification with objects manifest themselves as separation and therefore as suffering. It is essential to turn to the central belief that there is an entity separate from everything; beliefs, descriptions, history, ideas, that "I" exists as something real and concrete. Here Buddha completely dismantles these illusions clearly stating that "I" is empty, as do all the mystics, masters, enlightened beings, all those who have explored with dedication and passion the nature of the central identity of personality.

It is at this point that a shift from "searching for the center" to "centering" becomes possible in the seeker. This shift opens our attention by focusing it with the precision of the laser not only on the subject who is aware, rather than on the objects of their awareness, but also on their own nature: Who is in?

This openness and the intention that sustains it set in motion a dynamic and subtle process of dissolution of identification with the conventional self (ego) and with the separation that it continues to create and nourish.

Centering means then maintaining simultaneously the capacity for self-reflection in the awareness of the subject who experiences the objects as well as the complete identity/non-separation between subject and object – that is with becoming and being at the same time. Continuous and passionate inquiry with the Koan literally burns the barriers we have artificially created between the periphery and the center, and we begin to make our way into the understanding that each boundary is just an interpretation. We can see it as something that separates one phenomenon from another, an object from another or an object from the subject, or we can see it and feel it as the meeting point, a merging; a dynamic field of continuity, a continuum where it is impossible to determine end and beginning; where the subject exists in complete identity with the object he or she experiences. Where I am every breath, every heartbeat, every gust of wind, every sound, every thought and feeling. Where the absolute identity of the subject is ALL THERE IS. This is the manifesting of the real as a paradox: since the subject is empty every moment is absolutely full.

This is one of Buddha's most difficult statements to comprehend: "emptiness is fullness and fullness is emptiness".

This seemingly absurd phrase can only be understood through direct experience, even though modern science, and quantum physics, is at this point wonderfully approaching the possibility of demonstrating its profound truth.

Centering then becomes remembrance; remembrance of the subject, remembrance of emptiness, inclusion of all that is and transcendence.

As this may seem complex, I invite you to do an experiment with me for a moment. Close your eyes and put a hand on a thigh and feel what comes to you, temperature, pressure, contact, various sensations in your hand and leg; try to focus on that contact and not move on thinking or commenting and, if you do, simply include that movement and that thinking in your experience as well. The "normal" description of what you're doing is: "my hand is feeling the thigh through this contact". Now notice, is there a point where your hand ends and the contact begins? Or is it one unified experience? Observe, is there a point where the contact ends and the leg begins? Or is it one unified experience? Is there a point where the hand ends and the feeling begins?

Soon, as you watch you will find that the boundaries which seem to define the separation between subject and object, periphery and center are only descriptive names belonging to language but not to direct experience.

Reality is not only undivided but also indivisible.

Infinite diversity in infinite combinations

We are men and our lot in life is to learn and to be hurled into inconceivable new worlds.
Don Juan Matus, Yaqui warrior/sorcerer

Kabir, a great Indian mystic, expressed the paradox of unity/ diversity intrinsic to our True Nature very simply.

We are, he said, all different vases in shape and appearance and all made of the same mud, the mud of consciousness.

Unique and identical at the same time, identical in being all manifestations of universal consciousness and different in the uniqueness in which this consciousness manifests itself.

Osho, another great mystic, said that nature does not create carbon copies, each manifestation is unique and unrepeatable. And like them, hundreds of enlightened people have said the same thing for centuries.

This simple observation is absolutely central to our future, to the future of all humanity, if our species is to survive.

Diversity, difference, seen as manifestations of nature's incredible abundance and creativity, are the gateway to overcoming conflicts, inside ourselves and outside.

Five minutes (2)

2:09 a.m.

Who is in?

Pause and… Who is in? Settling down, slowing down, feeling and listening… outside there are noises… probably cars on the nearby highway and the thought why do I hear them so clearly? The wind probably moves from the land to sea…

Who is in? Sigh. I feel suspended. Who is in is suspended, and every word comes out with an internal distance like the one between one key and the next. There is inside a movement of the attention towards the clock but without ending up looking at it. I don't look at it. I am… I don't know. The breath comes out slow, I'm arriving here, and my fingers move slowly feeling with more strength and precision the keys that I now start tapping with more rhythm and with passion. I remember a movie *Finding Forrester*, where Sean Connery told his student to hit the keys of the typewriter hard, the feeling is quite different, there is a kind of wild intensity and a concentration that shakes with a movement of the head and noticing the shadow of the same that covers part of the keyboard… I'm here and I wonder what the fuck will those who read care about all this… I don't know and I can't know, it's for me… I look at the clock and I'm amazed… 2:19 a.m.

Inquiry (2)

1. What are your associations with emptiness? How do you feel when you hear this word and let it penetrate you? What's the atmosphere inside you?

2. For five minutes communicate everything you are aware of without making any choice about what to communicate and what not. Practice what is called "choiceless awareness" and note if there is resistance, doubt, tension, judgment, and also communicate all this immediately as soon as you are aware of it. Once finished look at what you feel in the body and what your inner atmosphere is.

3. Explore this phrase and how you interpret and understand it: The perennial movement of creation/evolution where the subject continually becomes the object of the new subject.

4. Explore your associations, ideas and concepts with respect to Spiritual Awakening. Do you have expectations? Do you think it's possible in general and specifically for you?

5. Central to our identification with Ego is the idea that "I am the doer". Explore this belief and how it manifests itself in your daily life. What are the most obvious effects of identifying yourself with doing?

6. Explore the question of "effort". What might happen to you if you stop trying? What are the possible catastrophes and jewels? Can you even imagine an effortless life? What are your most obvious associations with this word and in what relationship do they stand with your conditioning? What's going on in the body as you explore?

7. Who am I if I don't do? If I do not produce, if I do not manifest myself through the achievement of goals, the planning of programs for the future, competition with others?

8. What is the point of my life when time and space are determined not by external factors but by my presence?

From my ability to be here/now?

9. Who am I if the social labels I typically define myself with don't work? If I can't go around showing off the new car, the signed purse, my jewelry, or cheering for my favorite team?

10. Explore your ideas and experiences with respect to 1. Be centered; 2. Be lost. Note first of all if you contrast being centered and getting lost, how you do it and what effects it has in everyday life.

Three

If you open your mouth, you're already dead

When the restrictions you have don't limit you, this is what we mean by practice.
Shunryu Suzuki, mystic

I'm communicating.

The Koan is in, where it naturally resides.

The Koan in fact was never out because inside and outside don't exist.

I am communicating and words are not words, they are sounds, vessels of Being, embodied here/now, showing itself, taking shape, knowing itself and making itself known, revealing itself, to itself.

I am communicating and all masters, past, present and future utter these sounds that are the living Koan.

I am communicating and all sounds cross these apparent boundaries now transparent in an expansion that is meaningless, nor significant, nor expansive either, other than in the poverty of the words that are using me.

"Who says words with my mouth?" Rumi holds my hand and I'm his hand holding nothing.

This sweet pain of saying.

This silent and tender languor that fills every cell and flows contentedly into the blood of this body that only exists as the imagination of who is in...

Living without preferences

You will receive everything you need when you stop asking for what you do not need.

Nisargadatta Maharaj, mystic

And just hearing this, most people go into reaction and defence. "What! without MY preferences? So, where does MY freedom go?" And so on... It is a provocative title this one. It activates defensiveness and above all our ideas and concepts regarding individual freedom as well as our belief, conscious or not, that what we like and do not like define who we are.

Traveling around the world you can't imagine how many Italians I met who suffered and could not enjoy because of what they had to eat in India or Thailand or Germany. For them only Italian food was special, good and edible.

Most people seem compulsively obliged to proudly reaffirm and defend their preferences, completely oblivious to their attachment and dependence on them. Willing to fight and fight to assert those preferences as if their lives depended on them. And it is: that of their ego.

In Satori retreats, understanding the need to go beyond preferences is a fundamental step towards what we call the direct experience of oneself and the world in which we live.

It is not an easy or immediately obvious passage, and above all, it is something against which the ego absolutely rebels because intuitively it knows that letting go of our preferences means letting go of our personal history, our certainties and the control that we believe we exercise over our lives which we call freedom.

Attachment to likes and dislikes in all its countless forms: politics, cuisine, sex, landscape, architectural style, cinema, fashion, etc., is probably one of the fundamental causes of our difficulty in growing up and thus results in widespread narcissistic infantilism.

This is the benevolent form, excluding the positions expressed with aggressiveness and righteousness: "this sucks", "this is disgusting", "that is inconceivable", etc. This is also referred to by developmental psychology when it argues the average age of the majority of humans being at around six, seven years. This, coincidentally, is also the age in which the internal structuring of the inner judge and its dynamics of control tend to be completed.

And we are willing to do everything, including apply a fake sense of humor, to avoid looking at this attachment that has all the characteristics of a real ADDICTION.

It is difficult and shocking to recognize how our sense of identity is based on these platitudes: what we eat, the car we drive, the handbag or shoes we wear, the team we cheer for, the TV we watch... and our rejection, disdain or contempt for what is different.

It doesn't matter if we judge and look down from the top of our BMWs or our little Honda, our $300 bottle of whisky or our veganism: Prejudice – based on our preferences – is not just an idea but a continuous and habitual process of exclusion aimed at strengthening, confirming and nurturing our egoic identity and our need to feel special.

Living without preferences DOES NOT MEAN NOT HAVING PREFERENCES, it simply means recognizing the habitual and often compulsive nature of our preferences and checking if they correspond to who we are NOW, as they are generally an accumulation of the past. But above all it means understanding how our preferences inevitably imply a CONTRACTION IN THE FIELD OF POSSIBILITIES available to us in the present moment. Without our noticing, our likes and dislikes cripple the reality that manifests itself as new and unpredictable every moment locking us in a repetitive energy field, as it completely denies EROS, the spark of the new.

Each moment in fact presents itself with two fundamental aspects: on the one hand the past and the possibility to repeat it (reinforcing Karma accordingly) and on the other Eros, the spark of novelty, unpredictable and creative.

When we are present, we have the opportunity to consciously recognize both these components and, without ideologically excluding our preferences, we also have the opportunity to transcend them, momentarily or permanently, by opening ourselves up to Eros. Without this awareness, we are obliged to repeat the past glorifying our "virtuous coherence", while we are simply embroiled in a web of dependence devoid of freedom, slaves of our preferences.

Freeing ourselves from this slavery involves becoming aware of our preferences and doing so with compassion, without creating monsters and without rejecting the fact that preferences exist. At the same time seeing whether and how they correspond or not to who we are now, whether or not they help us to be present with everything that manifests here/now, or whether they close the field of possibilities.

Ultimately, awareness has to do with the ability to continuously include new perspectives by letting GO OF EXCLUSIVE ATTACHMENT to the old perspectives (not the perspectives themselves necessarily), in an interminable process of inclusion and transcendence, shining with creative power.

The jackal

Whenever I think about thinking, my thoughts become words. It is language talking to me. But the language came from outside. I think I control it, but it controls me back... language becomes part of the background noise, the air I breathe, gravity; it's just there... Language shapes us without our understanding how we are being shaped.
Orson Scott Card, author

And the most useful story of all is the one we repeat to ourselves for years and years: our personal history.

We have built it with attention to detail and a precise edition that has selectively excluded everything that does not belong to history as we want to remember it. After all, it's a matter of survival, is it not?

Our personal history is the dress that we wear all the time, even in a dream, and the composite of all the information that gels together in our social and internal images, in how we think, feel and evaluate ourselves outside and inside.

I don't know if you've ever wondered about the veracity of your story and how it is fundamental to your functioning in everyday life. In any case, when you begin to seriously ask yourself: Who is in? Or who am I? at some point it becomes almost inevitable that the story will end up under the magnifying glass. I said "almost inevitable" because of course there are many ways to avoid this exploration when we realize that the story we tell ourselves and that we continue to nourish day after day is the foundation of our identity.

Our personal history gives us a sense of continuity over time.

History gives us keys to interpretation of our past.

History gives us tools with which to evaluate the present.

History defines and justifies our values today, our beliefs, our opinions and above all our attachment to all this.

History makes us right.

When I ask myself, "Who is in?" history is the fundamental ground of our internal narrative and its communication. "Who is in?" finds definition and raison d'etre through that narrative, through all the myriad images and memories of themselves accumulated and condensed over time, and these images and memories emerge like air bubbles in liquid. They have the same consistency, just as they come to the surface, they burst revealing their emptiness.

Who is in? It is a boy or a girl? Is he a son? Is she a wife? Is he a citizen? Does he have a race? A nationality, an age? Who is in? Is he the color of his skin? Who is in? Is he spirit, matter, a body? Who is in? Does he have a mind? Does he have emotions?

Is who is in the one who acts? Is who is in asking for all of this?

Our habitual attachment to our personal history serves us by allowing us to hide from the questions and the terror that they can generate if we only begin to realize that we do not have a shred of the answers... but we do have the fixed ones, brooded, chewed over from our history.

Tibetans use a very effective metaphor to point attention to the distorted relation we have with our history and the way we deal with it: they say that we carry a corpse on one shoulder, our interpretation of the past, and when life presents itself in its unpredictability and uncertainty, we choose the habit of survival, and we give the corpse a small bite... to survive.

Adoration

Because I don't adore myself, then I adorn myself.
O, the young heroine in Beasts by D. Winslow

There is a discourse given by Osho, beautiful in its simplicity and precision, where he uses the metaphor of peeling an onion to make the listener understand the practice of self-exploration in the unveiling of the truth.

The love for truth manifests itself for a long time through a process of "unveiling": layer by layer we unveil ourselves, until there is nothing left to unveil and, as we fall in pure subjectivity, "Who is in" is naked, in its paradoxical nature of presence/absence.

This process is inherently painful because it is a deep spiritual surgery made even more intense by the concrete coincidence of surgeon and patient: you are the surgeon, and you are the patient. Most of us begin the operation by "peeling" the outer layers of our personality, those of everyday life: certain behaviors, certain beliefs, certain defences and forms of reactivity, certain words, certain survival strategies that are now obsolete and clearly an impediment to our growth and our ability to live a life more aligned with who we are in the present.

The more we go in, the more the unveiling comes alive. It becomes intimate, burning, unexpected, illuminating, essential and sometimes completely shocking. We have now learned to use the scalpel and, although fearful, intuitively we know where to cut. We also have a familiar contact with the love of truth that guides our attention as well as a sharp and precise awareness like a laser, and the Koan, "Who is in?"

For those who have never worked with an existential Koan or even with the classic ones of the Zen Rinzai tradition, it is difficult to even imagine how a single question can upset the habitual world and throw away our well-cultivated certainties, but this is exactly what happens.

The Koan attacks the mechanisms, strategies, mental habits through which we continually and futilely try to create certainty in daily life. It attacks our ideas with respect to time and space. It attacks the idea that the law of causality can be applied to every aspect of our experience. It undermines the need for meaning and deletes the need for the answer.

The Koan challenges our concepts and beliefs, our opinions and points of view, our ways of relating and thinking about the world. And it does so in simple and radically innocent ways.

A phrase we often use when working with Koans like "Who is in?" or "Who Am I?" is that we learn to live in a constant identity crisis.

And this is the big leap: after spending years and lots of energy trying to refine and improve the periphery of our personality, at some point, almost inevitably, we find ourselves facing the central question. This is the identity; "WHO" is at the center of the personality and the constant referent of all experiences, thoughts, emotions, sensations, perceptions, interactions and relationships?

In many mystical schools this moment is described as

"looking into the abyss". We've been going around for years, decades, maybe whole lives, patching here and there, putting a band-aid somewhere else, polishing what in the Sufi tradition is called the False Pearl, the image we present to the world that helped us survive in the world. At what price?! Then one day we can no longer hide and run away, avoid and delude ourselves, and understanding takes our breath away: "I AM NOT TRUE!"

Now adorning us is no longer enough. The image of ourselves and our images of the world begin to liquefy and show themselves for what they are: fictions, shadows of the past.

We feel thirsty. We burn with thirst. Thirst for honesty. Thirsty for truth. Thirsty for reality.

We realize that we are on the edge of the abyss and in that darkness there is no visible or perceptible bottom, there are no boundaries or dimensions, there is no direction, there is nothing, only the Koan: "Who is in?" And slowly we feel we fall into the abyss.

Meditating the universe

The true purpose [of Zen] is to see things as they are, to observe things as they are, and to let everything go as it goes... Zen practice is to open up our small mind.
Shunryu Suzuki, mystic

I was about sixteen when I first tried to meditate. I was reading a book about Yoga that a friend had lent me and I was intrigued by the technique of closing my eyes and following my breath.

For a couple of nights, while everyone was sleeping, I sat on my bed and tried to meditate, and in amazement I noticed something was happening! Everything slowed down inside as my attention focused on breathing and the boundaries of the physical body became less solid; it was exciting, surprising, intriguing. Until on the third night, in this inner space that opened up, some parts of my body began to quiver and shake out of control, and I got afraid and decided to stop the experiment. It was many years later that I discovered that these were tensions that, so to speak, were "unscrewing themselves" and that my body had begun to do exactly what was needed. The lack of control scared me.

When we surrender in the practice of meditation and let go of control and stop "doing" it often happens that a natural intelligence takes over and begins to open our physical, and also our subtle, body. The experience which we are generally accustomed to which is made up of familiar sensations, more or less known emotions and a seemingly uninterrupted flow of thoughts, begins to unravel. And that can generate fear. Don't worry, it's both natural and healthy that this happens.

The world in which we live is supported and justified by our identification with internal structures: a range of images, concepts and interpretations solidified over time that are filters which compulsively force us to repeat how we experience ourselves and the world within often within narrow parameters. In meditation, especially as we meditate surrendering to everything that is moment to moment, our internal structures and representations tend to become more fluid, less rigid, less certain, more transparent, less mandatory, less compulsive.

For example, we begin to realize how rarely we have the direct experience of a particular object, a flower, a perfume, a feeling, etc., as we immediately shift our attention from the object itself to the name, the label we give it and other associations. In this movement, a few things happen:

Our attention shifts from feeling to thinking, that is, from the heart or belly to the head.

Each name is associated with memories, and therefore we move from the present to the past and "think" the object through comparison and evaluation.

Evaluation and comparison involve a hierarchy of values that has been created over time and that includes beliefs, judgments, prejudices, conditioning in general.

The result is that we completely lose the connection with the specific object, in this specific present, and also our freedom to be here/now.

One of the effects of meditating is to clearly reveal this mode of operation, and to open ourselves to experiences without past, without evaluations, without beliefs, without judgments... even without names. Right now, you are reading, and your eyes follow the signs of words, but your experience exists in itself even if you forget the words. If you do not assign any label or meaning to the experience, the experience is "a priori" with respect to the definition and the meaning you give it.

And what if you went deep to experience what it is to read? What are the eyes that follow the signs? What are the concepts you use to interpret? At some point in your meditation all definitions and the attempt to understand disappear, and what remains are the fundamental elements of this universe: matter, energy and awareness. And you are meditating the universe, and the universe is meditating you. And it's pure ecstasy.

Five minutes (3)

5:12 p.m.

Who is in?

I am sitting outdoors, and the crow makes itself heard along with other birds and insects. Inside there is me who feels, notices, receives, recognizes the attention that moves and the wind. I feel the cool of the lake and the soft grass under my feet. I breathe deeply and the wind rises along with my breath and I smile, and I am present here with everything around me that is inside. I am reminded of a question in the Dharma Combat (*) about inside and outside and the trap opening. I look at the clock and I have time... So... So... just feeling, welcoming, merging with... I look up and see the lake and the grass moving... I am breath and beauty.

5:17 p.m.

*The Dharma Combat is a technique used in Zen to introduce a student to the practice of Koans. In this technique the master attacks the student's mind with simple questions that hide a trap aimed at destructuring specific aspects of the common mind based on duality.

For example, I ask you, "Are the words you're reading inside or outside of your mind? If you tell me they are inside, I'll hit you thirty times; if you tell me outside, I'll send you to hell without doors. Tell me, where are the words you are reading?"

When the student has had the direct experience of reality and grasped the basic understandings that are non-rational, logical and linear then the master begins with the traditional Koans. Some of them are quite famous: "What was your face before your mother was born?" "What is the sound of one hand clapping?" "Tell me why Bodhidharma went to the East?"... There are more than a thousand of them, collected in ten families and each family has a gate. When the student passes a gate a specific structure that occupies the common mind is seen, becomes transparent and is passed through.

Each Koan has only two possible answers based on the same understanding: one answer is correct and ordinary, and the other is correct and poetic. Beauty and elegance are central to the practice of Koans.

Inquiry (3)

1. What relationship do you have with your preferences? Are you attached to them? If so, how does this attachment manifest itself? Try to be detailed and concrete by exploring the various fields of your life. Do so without judging and noting which preferences you are most attached to. Notice

if you feel this attachment in a particular area of the body.

2. Preferences and addiction. This is an extremely difficult topic to address because one of the most definitive features of any addiction is self-deception and deep resistance to admitting to ourselves that we are addicted. Move with caution and curiosity, with affection and honesty.

3. Bring to mind situations where you had a clear perception of pretending and the ways you justified it. How did you feel about doing it: powerful; dirty; helpless; obligatory; confused? Note whatever comes. See if you have any idea how and where you learned it's dangerous to be true?

4. Explore situations, events where you felt real. What sensations, emotions, thought-forms, energy qualities were present?

5. Exercise: Sit comfortably and visualize yourself as you described yourself in exploration #3 – feeling fake – in front of you on your left, and as you described yourself in exploration #4 – feeling true – in front of you on the right. With your eyes open, include both images at the same time knowingly. When you feel ready say aloud: I AM BOTH and notice what happens in your body; if and how your internal atmosphere changes. Write about this experience. Practice this exercise regularly.

6. Alone or with someone else; in front of a mirror or a picture of a master. Practice "Awareness without choice"; let yourself communicate aloud in a constant flow what comes to awareness, whatever it is. The continuous movement of objects that appear and disappear and your attention that notices their presence. Include everything, without choosing anything: thoughts, sensations, images, emotions, perceptions, moods, memories, energy or physical movements... simply communicate what you are aware of... communicate judgments, resistances, doubt, space, silence, joy, fear, passion... EVERYTHING, WITHOUT CHOICE.

7. Explore the theme of control. What are your ideas, beliefs, prejudices, associations with this word?

8. Explore control in different aspects of your life and in your daily functioning. Avoid self-judgment and look at the control you operate within in a dispassionate way, as a scientist or yourself. We've all learned to control, look how you do it: strategies, modes, situations, areas in your body... Do not fall into the trap of guilt or self-deception.

9. Bring to mind events where you've lost or let go of control: feel the quality and effects.

Four

The practice of surrendering in meditation

Surrender is the flowering of the understanding that ego doesn't exist.
Osho, mystic

The question of surrender was, and is, the focus of my spiritual journey in a very personal way since the first name that Osho gave me – Samarpan – means precisely surrender. I remember well when I received it at Rajneeshpuram in Oregon and the sensations that burst into me as I heard the meaning of that name. The first was, "He caught me! How can he give me such a name, to me, a warrior – surrender!?" and then a sense of inevitability, acceptance, excitement and... surrender. That name, and above all its meaning, was a wedge planted in the center of my self-image, both the one inside and the one I had presented to the world for years and years.

From that moment on Osho accompanied and guided me in recognizing something that had been already manifesting itself for some time in my life: my capacity to understand the need to surrender and the will to do so.

I certainly did not expect that, by that name, the direction would be indicated with absolute precision and, above all, the adventure of discovering moment by moment what it was to surrender concretely and how surrendering was inextricably linked for me with the need to experience my vulnerability.

Surrender is a word that for almost everyone has negative connotations, associated images of defeat and humiliation, cowardice and loss. This is what they have taught us and the powerful shadow that lives in our unconscious and, from what I have seen around, it does not seem to me that any religious idealization has in any way really affected this shadow in the vast majority of human beings.

Surrendering spiritually is on the other hand mostly understood in a fatalistic way, as a helpless acceptance of everything that happens to us, being a humble and obedient victim hopeful for salvation. And so, we find ourselves incapacitated between two interpretations that, both, completely deny our humanity and the intelligence of True Nature: demonization on the one hand and idealization on the other.

So, what is my understanding of surrender? What am I talking about? What does it mean to practice surrendering consciously?

I start from the spiritual aspect and then I'll come to everyday life.

Surrendering spiritually basically means letting go of control. The control we try to compulsively exert on our experience. Experience consists of sensations, feelings, emotions, thoughts and moods, and surrendering means recognizing the continuous manifesting and change of all these elements that continuously flow, WITHOUT INTERFERING IN ANY WAY to change them, to manipulate them, to reject them, to assimilate them, to understand them, to box them.

Surrender is then synonymous with awareness without choice, without preference and without effort. Surrendering is the natural effect of understanding that there is no separate self that can control what it feels, sees, thinks, perceives. Surrendering is therefore a getting out of the way by letting life flow in its creative complexity and intrinsic unity.

In daily life surrender means responding to the present moment from the totality of complexity and intrinsic unity, without excluding anything. It means that we include our preferences, our shadows, our shortcomings, our beauty, our intelligence, our cowardice and our splendor. It means that we manifest more and more intensely the totality that we learn to recognize through our practice of meditation as we let go of control and, above all, of the illusion that there is an ego that can control. In everyday life we make choices, we operate, we function, and all this begins to take place from an inner state of integration and inclusion of everything that is MOMENT BY MOMENT in a way that is flexible and open to the mystery of Being that manifests itself continuously.

This is practice. This is practice in meditation. This is the practice of awakened consciousness that alone can know itself without controlling because the ego, by its constitution, can only exist in separation and therefore MUST strive to control. When we practice letting go of control in meditating, we open the door to our Already Awakened Consciousness, embodying this consciousness in the present of meditation.

Surrendering in the practice of meditation means, for a start, meditating without a goal to be achieved, a purpose, without wanting anything from meditation and without needing anything special as an effect of our practice.

We do not meditate TO improve ourselves, TO be more aware, TO get enlightened, TO solve our problems but rather we meditate FROM AND IN the full and complete inclusion of everything that is, moment to moment. FROM AND IN the concrete recognition that if I surrender to all that is every moment naturally the compulsion to control fades and then disappears. Meditation is surrender by letting go of control over our experience in the present moment and simply being present with everything that is in the continuous and unpredictable flow of change.

When we meditate, we get OUT of the way and let life be exactly as it is. No control is surrender and inclusion and integration of the totality that we are, and this totality manifests itself as intelligence, intuition, strength, clarity, tenderness, beauty, love and truth, and all the flowering of Being.

Another element that creates confusion in meditators is the

idea that to surrender I have to do something. Surrendering IS NOT A DOING BECAUSE THERE IS NO DOER; it is a delusion we carry with us that there exists a separate doer. And so, the answer everyone gives to the question, WHO AM I? It is the definition of a doing, a function, a role: I am a doctor, a teacher, a mother, a man, a seeker, a mystic, etc., etc. Surrender is STOPPING DOING, it is a DIRECT EXPERIENCE that there is no separate self and that there is nothing to do and that everything already happens on its own and that we are immersed in all there is, and we are also an inseparable part of it, the realization of, "I AM ALL THERE IS."

The whole of society and culture is based on the belief that I have to do something to be someone while Being is "a priori" to any doing and is "always and already". And this was the coup de grace (in the truest sense of the word) that Osho gave me my second name – Avikal – which means quiet, serene, non-action, as well as the one who is already at home.

This conscious non-doing is at the center of surrendering, and meditation is the practice of not doing in complete surrender to all that is. So, my invitation is to take about fifteen, twenty minutes whenever you can, sit in a comfortable position that allows you to stay alert and stop doing completely: don't look, don't interpret, don't change anything, don't hope, don't check, just stop and stay with yourself letting everything be included, thoughts, hopes, interpretations, etc., consciously without choice. And in this way you are already at home, you are already complete, you are already awakened and free.

Curiosity, curiosity, curiosity!

I don't have any special talents, I'm just passionately curious.
Albert Einstein, scientist

In the Awareness Intensive Retreats that our institute offers

– Who is in? (three-day format) and Satori (seven days) – participants work with questions that are known as existential Koans. Koan is a Japanese word that indicates a question that cannot be answered intellectually but of which you can have direct experience, such as Who is in? Who am I? What is love? What is life? What is freedom? etc. The initial and main step in asking these questions is learning to focus our own intention. We do this by keeping in mind – with as much constancy and intensity as possible – the question we're working on and the instruction that's given is: Keep the Koan inside all the time.

This technique undoubtedly works. I have verified it with thousands of people and myself, and the understanding that undergoes it is very simple: IF THE ANSWER DID NOT ALREADY EXIST IN THE UNIVERSE, THE POSSIBILITY OF DOING THE EXPERIENCE, THERE WOULD NOT BE THE QUESTION.

When we bring this understanding into everyday life, we can use it to activate a simple practice based on finding what is the main question, or questions, that concerns me at this stage of my life and consciously activate it and then keep it in mind as intensely and often as possible. Here, now, I'm no longer talking about "existential" Koans but personal questions that directly and specifically concern me, things like, what's the job I really want to do? How can I love without fear? How can I realize my potential as a writer? What prevents abundance in my life? etc.

There are a couple of things you need to be aware of:

1. Through our inquiry we are engaging one of the fundamental forces of the universe: THE DYNAMIC THRUST OF CREATIVITY and to make it powerful, the closer the question is to our heart, the more intimate and truer it is, the stronger our intention and the energy field we create. So, if you want to know the price of shoes or where to rent a car or where to buy organic food it

is easier and faster to go to Google (and also the Net is obviously a manifestation of universal creativity…).

2. Don't worry about the answer. The usual and compulsive habit learned from family, school and society, is TO GIVE ANSWERS AT ALL COSTS TO PROVE THAT WE KNOW. Here, however, we are solely focused on inquiring, and let existence give us the elements we need, and they may be very different from those we have learned to imagine or can see from our limited present point of view.

Keep the question inside: in your mind, heart and belly

As you keep your question present – and at first, I suggest you practice only with one – you'll begin to notice the spontaneous onset of feelings, or images, or memories, thoughts, words, and concepts (or even all these things) that, often not even knowing how, you'll feel connected to what you're asking for. As I wrote above: don't stick to anything in the search for a hasty answer. Stay alert and above all stay OPEN.

Maintaining an OPEN FIELD AND SUBSTANTIAL AVAILABILITY TO ALL THAT IS, is the other side of this technique; in doing so you move, gently and firmly, away from the structure of your personality that is defined and held together by a frozen collection of interpretations, beliefs, judgments, prejudices and inherited values. This structure made of boundaries can only repeat itself as it has done countless times so far, annihilating the intuition and brilliance of the intelligence of your True Nature.

When YOU DO NOT GRASP OR REJECT what appears in your awareness, at some point you will start noticing filaments of light, meaning, energy, perception, feeling, that will begin connecting those specific objects that have been raised in your awareness in relation to the question. Until one day – when you are not even waiting – suddenly everything will come together to form a pattern, simple, obvious, intensely clear, intimate, full of kind love and your answer will be there, evident, and there will be no doubt.

All this has to do with DIRECT KNOWING.

This is where INTENTION, the male side, Yang, of this technique, and OPENING, the feminine side, Yin, intersect. The center point of the cross between the horizontal space/time dimension and the vertical dimension of the interiority here/now.

And at this point DIVINE MIND is manifesting itself as GRACE.

The two sides of the technique complement and support each other. The more unwavering your intention to keep the question in mind, the more your openness tends to include. The more relaxed your opening, the more intense will be your intention.

Stay open, without grasping or rejecting

The inner attitude in this practice is what I often refer to as "OPEN INQUIRY". This essentially means staying in touch with curiosity as the engine of the investigation, not looking at all costs for an answer, and learning to be present with information that appears in your consciousness without hastily putting it in order. Which means not falling into the trap of the mind "who believes it knows and wants to control reality through knowledge". Everything you know obviously belongs to the past and the open investigation takes place in the present and, without discarding what you know from the past, is open, precisely, to new understandings, revelations, insights, surprises.

We learn to be present with the different dimensions of our experience without interfering and manipulating it while contacting a familiar physical tension. Practice begins with connecting with a well-known physical tension. Well known in the sense that it is a tension that, more than any other, is familiar to you, that repeats itself, that has been there for a long time, that perhaps you have tried to dissolve many times without succeeding. It can be in the solar plexus, on the shoulders, in the belly, in the throat, in the chest, in the genitals... anywhere in the body. The important thing is that when you feel it you recognize it, with that mixture of familiarity and frustration: No! Back again?!

1. Breathing slowly bring your attention to the tension, to FEEL IT, NOT TO ANALYZE IT... approach it as if you were approaching a puppy, kindly and gently... YOU WANT TO CREATE CONTACT, and feel it in all its dimensions. What kind of tension is it: a pressure? a density? a contraction? a hollow or a bulge? what color? what depth? Under the skin, in the muscles, the bones, the joints, etc.? Has it a shape, direction? STAY THERE AND FEEL, WITHOUT CHANGING ANYTHING... WITHOUT CHANGING ANYTHING...

2. When you start to feel that you are in contact with that tension and in a state of simple observation of the same, open your attention to other information that may be associated. For example, you may feel one or several related emotions; you may have associated thoughts and judgments; memories, images, other sensations in the body may come to light. Observe what comes up, WITHOUT GRASPING OR REJECTING, WITHOUT PUTTING ORDER, WITHOUT REACHING TO CONCLUSIONS...

3. Repeat these steps until the various inputs begin to connect spontaneously and a pattern begins to show containing meaning, feeling, intellectual understanding and a physical sensation as of a "thawing" of the tension. And this is precisely what happens: the tension is in

fact a frozenness that can only melt in the light of your presence, love and awareness.

4. You can apply this technique to any physical tension, at any time.

Opening to space will cause what I called a "thawing" of tension, its "opening up". What happens has to do, to be more precise, with the transformation of our perception of INNER SPACE.

Imagine this situation with me: you are in a room full of furniture and trinkets, all thrown one thing over the other. You are trying to understand what to do with it and orient yourself, and it seems impossible: there is too much of everything and it is chaotic and frustrating, and you jump from one thing to another, from one place to another, as we often do inside, from one thought to another, from one emotion to another, from one feeling to another, from one mood to another, from one image to another, from one perception to another, from one desire to another... nonstop and endless.

STOP! JUST STOP!

It becomes clear to you, now, that before you understand what's there you need to give it a rest, come back to yourself and stop chasing your tail. So, you stop somewhere in the room and take a landmark, let's say a particular pile of stuff. This is what you did when you focused on a familiar physical tension that keeps coming back, and you chose a physical tension BECAUSE TENSIONS IN THE BODY ARE THE DENSEST ELEMENTS OF OUR EXPERIENCE, while emotions, thoughts, moods are progressively becoming less dense, and it is more difficult to be present with them at the beginning.

The good news is that THE OBJECTS THAT CROWD OUR INNER SPACE ARE NOT MATERIAL AND therefore do not respond to the laws of physics, for example they can literally dissolve if we are present, we mirror them (mirror-like awareness) and recognize them (discriminating awareness). So, what starts to happen inside is that in feeling the familiar tension and the various things associated with it, this heap begins to melt away in the light of our awareness and our love – without grasping or rejecting – and A SENSE OF SPACIOUSNESS BEGINS TO MANIFEST ITSELF INSIDE as the forms dissolve.

> *Space appears when you are present with the different elements of the experience without grasping or rejecting. And as the individual objects dissolve, space opens up more and is "liberated" as a result of a fading of attachment to old interpretations. Do nothing, just be present and if you can also enjoy the opening of the inner space, it is fantastic!*

Space is the fundamental ground where all forms appear and disappear.

Understanding fear so we can return home – 1

Litany against Fear:
I must not fear. Fear is the mind-killer. Fear is the little death that brings total obliteration. I will face my fear. I will permit it to pass over me and through me. And when it has gone past, I will turn the inner eye to see its path.
Where the fear has gone there will be nothing. Only I will remain.
Frank Herbert, author

Living without fear is a process guided by intimacy, and that is the desire to know oneself by being oneself. Clear intent to tell myself the truth about myself.

Lack of intimacy is narcissism. Narcissism is not a pathology as they sell it to us but the general human condition in the forgetfulness of our true nature. Narcissism does not mean being compulsively interested in oneself but, on the contrary, not being able to practice self-reflection and introspection. It means absolute dependence on external reflections and therefore has to do with self-image. As long as we are dependent on external reflections we will inevitably be forced to live in fear and self-image. No intimacy, no truth, just ideas, opinions, points of view, beliefs.

Intimacy means being in contact with our fear, knowing it, recognizing it, savoring it, playing with it, fighting with it, chasing it, fleeing it, hugging it, pushing it away, including it, transcending it...

Fear in the heart

There are three types of fear: fear in the mind, fear in the heart and fear in the belly. They are very different from each other and each one of us has more difficulty with one type than with another. Mine has been fear in my heart for decades.

Fear in the heart has to do with the shadow of negative fusion with our mother and our attachment to images of frustrated love, lack of nourishment, desperate waiting, impossible intimacy, wounds so deep as to be incomprehensible, sticking to images of ourselves as unworthy of love and care.

Fear in the heart feeds on waiting to be hurt again.

Fear in the heart has to do with continuing to divide light (the good mother) from darkness (the bad mother) and believing in the eternal inevitability of this damn split.

Fear in the heart has to do with the tendency to fight against an existence that we continue to consider an enemy, antagonistic, cruel towards us.

Fear in the heart makes no sense, it has no dimension, it cannot be "rationally understood", it precedes the formation of ego and reason.

The Way: surrender to the present moment.

We let the wave transport us in its direction, and with passion and curiosity we ask ourselves in every situation, "What has this to do with me, what I see in the world, in the other, in events?"

We consciously practice, through self-inquiry, the union of the masculine (asking) and the feminine (receiving). We seek in the darkness with the light of our availability, affection, gentle determination. When shadow and light come together and the separation line becomes a merging line, fear in the heart goes away, little by little, until it disappears.

Fear in the mind

Fear in the mind is like a tick sucking on ideas that have been imprinted in us, and making them truthful and real beyond whether they match our direct experience or not. This tick loves to attach to three fears in particular: fear of the unknown, fear of death (with different variations: illness, madness, etc.), and fear of uncertainty.

Just as surrender is the main way to transcend fear in the heart, experiential understanding is for fear in the mind, and the most effective way to understand is to use self-inquiry by illuminating these fears with our awareness and existential intelligence. Why do I have these fears and what do I really know about what I assume I fear?

The unknown: wait a moment, if it is unknown, how can I be afraid of it? Isn't the unknown by definition something I have no experience of? Do I remember how as a child I was absolutely attracted and full of wonder towards the world in and around me? Towards my body? To my senses? Towards the different, the other...? Have I completely forgotten the excitement of curiosity and discovery? We were not born with the fear of what arises moment by moment and, even only intellectually, it is not difficult to recognize that this moment has never happened before. So, what justifies my fear is not the reality of this moment but my abandoning this moment and its experience by overlapping the past through some form of comparison-based assessment. What happened in the past takes the place of what's going on in the present. Result: automatic reactivity = compulsive repetition of the past.

Death: if you are reading, breathing, sensing your body and hearing the sounds around you it means that you are not dead. It also means that you don't know anything about death DIRECTLY but that you only have ideas, images, concepts, prejudices, all acquired. Fear of death is acquired by culture. Death is an absolutist concept that has taken the place of transformation. Energy cannot be created or destroyed, only transformed.

Perhaps you saw death, maybe you read about it, maybe you risked dying, maybe you touched it in someone else, but you're not dead. So, whatever you think you know about death is just interpretations, information, concepts, NOT EXPERIENCE. Then observe how those concepts, ideas, and interpretations reinforce a state of self-hypnosis that you call fear. In a large number of so-called "primitive" and ancient cultures, death was not at all scary because it was in no way associated with a fundamental separation, which is all cultural, between what we call life and what we call death. Fear of death is, in most cases, an excuse not to live by taking full responsibility, and glory, for our life force in all its manifestations. And finally, uncertainty. Although a desire for certainty and security in existential terms is more than understandable, here too it is a question of opening our eyes and acknowledging that the only certain element of every moment is change. Uncertainty is the warp and plot of life, and the real question is not how to avoid it but how to learn to be present in uncertainty without denying and demonizing it and, at the same time, learning to support ourselves in all ways: mental, energetic, emotional, spiritual. When we are present, we can see how what we call uncertainty is the uninterrupted flow of possibilities in infinite combinations and how our uniqueness expresses itself in our ability to support ourselves, moment after moment, at this moment, in this manifesting of the mystery of existence.

Here the creative capacity explodes.

Fear in the belly

A completely different thing. Fear in the belly has to do with the ability to act, with the question: will I make it? Perhaps the most paralyzing fear because there is no understanding or acceptance or self-belief or anything else that can answer this question except action itself and the experience of being in action. And the fundamental trap is not so much the question itself as the duality failure/success. As soon as we start to believe in the validity of this duality, we begin to get entangled with it by asking how we can make sure we succeed and avoid failure. You can see how this can lead to paralysis and procrastination.

In almost all mystical traditions there is a teaching that uses the symbolism of throwing oneself into an abyss, which points to letting go of control and expectation of a certain result, and affirms spontaneous, immediate, unpredictable action. Control means once again protection and repetition of the status quo, a belief that there is a real possibility of manipulating and guiding the future moment and bending existence to our will.

In the belly there is the Hara center, what is considered the center of Being, where life and death are ONE, where sound is silence, where doing is immobility, where being is becoming and emptiness is full. Where the paradox exists in absolute clarity and the opposites do not exist but are rather complementary, where failure is success and success is failure. Where every distinction appears for what it is: only mental image and description.

I DO NOT KNOW, the innocence of not knowing, the practice of not knowing shifts our attention from the dualism success/ failure and brings it back to its natural context: the totality of Being here/now, the presence that is expressed in pure existence as an action without goals, such as this writing, this breathing, this thinking, this feeling, my fingers touching the keys and the wind outside the window and the deep currents that underlie words. The fear in the belly dissolves moment by moment leaving room for the confidence that the belly itself responds directly and authentically to the present moment ENJOYING the lack of knowledge.

There was a Zen master who rarely spoke and answered every question using two dolls he held next to his seat. One was heavy in the head, and when he hit it, it fell on its face and got stuck there on the floor; the other was heavy in its belly and when the master gave it a shot it would fall, hit the floor and come back up.

Pointing at it, the master would say: This is enlightenment. This is Zen. You fall and you get up again, ten, a hundred, a thousand times, until falling is no longer a mistake or a failure. Only part of existence, such as wind, clouds, rain, light and darkness.

Understanding fear so we can return home – 2

Ego is not a thing but rather a subtle effort, and you can't use effort to get rid of effort – you end up with two efforts instead of one. The ego itself is a perfect manifestation of the Divine, and it is better to handle it by resting in Freedom than trying to get rid of it, which simply makes it stronger.
Ken Wilber, philosopher

Living without fear: centauric awareness

There are deep forces that push into our psyche, shake our bodies and stir emotions. Understanding our animal soul, its tendencies and desires is central to freeing ourselves from fear. Integrating the thrusts of this absolutely irrational part of our nature is a fundamental piece of the journey to recognizing our authenticity and uniqueness. Social, sexual and survival instincts are expressions of this soul and intrinsic manifestations of our belonging to the animal world. The distortions we carry within us prevent us not only from living our instincts but also from recognizing them in their naturalness and also in their limitation. By preventing ourselves from being animal, we deny the roots of our body, our soul and our place in the evolution of the universe. And we continue to separate spirit and matter and create that suffering that we say we want to let go of. But transcendence cannot take place through rejection and separation but only through the inclusion that is in the recognition of who I am, in the mystery that I am while revealing in all its forms, moment after moment, instinct after instinct, desire after desire, understanding after understanding. The courage of Being is born in the recognition of the complexity and uniqueness of my Being, in all its animal/human forms.

Living without fear: resistance

Living without fear means living without resistance to what is, or if you prefer, without preferences, Of course, I like bitter chocolate more than milk chocolate, but this does not mean condemning one chocolate idealizing the other... I am not dumb, what if I change tastes? Without resistance means without defences, without a priori exclusions, open to the moment that happens now, to the events that unfold in and around me... Every answer happens from the depths of the soul not from the periphery of personality and the soul is not afraid because it knows that it is all that it is while the personality is intrinsically paranoid because it knows that it is only a fiction, a mask that continually wonders: what if they discover me?

Living without fear is living without secrets, without hiding, without pretending to be something different from who I am, who you are, who we are. Our unconscious, this universe, have more than enough mysteries to reveal, we invite them to do so, then we will hear these words resound in our hearts: welcome to planet Earth.

Living without fear: presence

Living without fear is a PRACTICE: THE PRACTICE OF PRESENCE.

This is the recipe (then if you want you can add your own toppings):

1. When I feel what I call fear I stop and first throw away the FEAR label and keep my attention on recognizing the physical, mental, emotional symptoms, my inner atmosphere.
2. When I have mixed enough and the ingredients are familiar to me, I can see that, precisely, they are INGREDIENTS, they are the objects that, mixed all together, I have habitually called fear.
3. At this point I can see that there is the cook, I, the SUBJECT who is aware of all these OBJECTS.
4. And finally I can also recognize that the SUBJECT IS NOT THE OBJECTS.

This recipe has been well known in India for millennia under the name NETI NETI (neither this nor that).

A good cook PRACTICES, if not he does philosophy.

Living without fear: responsibility

To live without fear the fundamental step, and perhaps the most difficult, is recognizing, understanding and taking responsibility that WE CREATE the fear, as we make a vegetable soup. We make it in the literal sense that WE MATERIALLY CREATE fear.

There is a Zen story where the disciple goes to the master and asks him, "Master, what is death?" and the master replies, "You are already dead." What does that mean? It means that when we use words unconsciously, we unconsciously create the universe in which we live. The soup is made of ingredients, objects that mixed together give a final product with certain characteristics.

A good cook:

a. knows his ingredients,
b. knows how to use them creatively,
c. does not depend on them, it is they who serve him.

When we mechanically call our experience fear, stating without a moment's pause that fear is what we are feeling, we are bad cooks, we are slaves to a name and the past, we are disconnected from the ingredients and therefore from the experience of the present moment, and above all we are identified with the form (the name) and we have forgotten I AM (we are dead).

When I remember I AM, then I take responsibility for the world I'm creating and only then am I free.

Living without fear: Karma and Eros

When I mechanically label my experience, I concretely deny the fundamental reality of the universe, its indomitable, inevitable, incomprehensible and irrepressible creativity. Every moment we are faced with a new universe, completely and fundamentally different from the one we have just passed. In this new universe we are at a crossroads: on the one hand Karma and that is the accumulation of the past and the possibility of repeating it, and on the other Eros, the creative spark that every new moment contains.

Living without fear means first of all being aware of this crossroads and consciously choosing. Sometimes we will be led to repeat the past and identify with our Karma feeling the impotence that this choice entails, and we will experience freedom within the constraints imposed by the environment inside and outside. Other times we will have the courage to take risks and choose Eros and the unknown. There is no fair and definable way of making this choice a priori; it will depend on our presence and on the conditions under which this choice takes place. Awareness is everything.

Here I want to offer a concept that is also a practice: when we find ourselves at the crossroads I have described and fear tends by inertia to pull us towards Karma and the comfort zone to which we are accustomed, let's try to look the other way towards the possibility of taking a HEALTHY CREATIVE RISK. It is healthy when we take it being aware of our abilities and the possibility of expanding them, without hurting ourselves, or at least giving ourselves all the support possible to limit the chance of getting hurt.

It's creative when it moves us into a field of possibility larger than usual, there's a sense of excitement and innocence, and it's one step at a time, rooted in the here/now, which means there's no fixed end result to achieve.

Living without fear: contact

Aikido is a martial art that has informed and been a foundation of most of my practical understandings. For starters, AIKI means fusion, union, harmony, and DO is the way.

Already this was a clear invitation to look, even in situations of aggression, combat, conflict, separation, for the higher way that would take me beyond. There is in particular a central concept to this art that defines its practice: KIMUSUBI = to join one's own life force (KI) with that of the other. It is the simple statement that in every situation the most intelligent, efficient and effective way to go beyond separation (conflict) is consciously seeking contact. Physical, emotional, mental and spiritual contact.

If we look at fear carefully, we will see clearly that one of its central features is isolation, distance from me, from the other and from the environment, a deep contraction of the energy field, a shrinking and a tightening of borders. There is no contact, first of all with myself, and there is no intimacy.

In Aikido all techniques are based on getting in touch, seeking contact, establishing contact, with clear experience in the body that every time the contact breaks and I move away, there is pain. Physical above all, but also mental (anxiety), emotional (frustration) and spiritual (sense of futility and loss).

Contact is evolutionarily an incredible leap in quality to go beyond the compulsivity of automatic reactions to fear: struggle, escape, freezing. I stop and try to make contact with me. And then with the other. I literally come closer within and without. I risk the vulnerability of intimacy.

One day a monk meeting Dogen, a Zen master, asked him, "Master, what's under your robe?" This question was a ritual way of asking what enlightenment is, and Dogen replied: "Deep intimacy."

Contact is the practical art that discovers this intimacy, every moment, in every situation, with every other. And it all starts here, with yourself.

Living without fear: recognizing and cultivating our multiple intelligences

Neuroscience has been discovering and legitimizing in the last twenty years what mystics and many premodern cultures have known for millennia and that is that every human being has not only the brain that we are used to calling such, that in the head, but also one in the heart and belly. Both the heart and the belly are in fact full of neurons and, when we say things like: "I feel it in the heart" or "I move from the belly," they are not only metaphorical expressions but reflect forms of intelligence that take place in those energy centers. Most people are unaware of what are now commonly called multiple intelligences and continue to think that the only intelligence is cognitive/intellectual intelligence. Reality is that we continually "know the world" through a multitude of resources and that, of course, the more we are in contact with these resources, recognize and develop them, the broader and more precise our experience of ourselves and of the whole reality in which we live. These intelligences are also those that allow us to get in touch and respond creatively to what happens in the present rather than reacting automatically through fight, flight and freezing.

Emotional intelligence, kinesthetic intelligence, aesthetic intelligence, interpersonal intelligence, spiritual intelligence... they are just some of our potentials and the foundations of our individual freedom and liberation from fear and repetition of the past.

Let us also remember that by freeing ourselves we are giving a concrete message to others that liberation is possible and with it a new real humanity.

Presence is the natural state of every human being

Completeness is the experience of "I am" without mind. Without anyone reflecting it and saying, "I am," without subjectivity. It's just the current "being here," without the conceptualization of the mind. "I am" is the same thing as presence, like "I", like true identity, only there is no need to conceptualize.
A.H. Almaas, mystic and author

Presence is simply the natural and spontaneous manifestation of awareness existing moment after moment. We have no choice whether to be aware or not: awareness is our nature and manifests itself indirectly through an apparent continuum of objects of awareness. These objects can be internal – such as thoughts, emotions, perceptions, sensations – or external, and between them there is not an essential difference, but only of density. They are all impressions in awareness, waves in the ocean, objective awareness.

This awareness that I am, that you are, is impersonal and not possessed or possessable. It's timeless and nameless. Without boundaries, color or religion. It's not social or ethical or moral. This awareness makes up your bones, your blood, your brain, the eyes that read, the words that flow and the meaning you give them and the effect they have in your heart or belly. This awareness does not come and go, it is always here, it is always now.

When you think you're not aware, awareness is aware of that thought. You can't escape your nature. Ego exists in the illusion of being separated from consciousness: the famous fish that asks where the ocean is while swimming in it. Awareness of the ego and its alleged separation is there at that moment.

It doesn't exist, it can't exist, a moment without awareness. What confuses us is the mental recognition of, "I am aware." It takes place in opposition to moments of nonrecognition and therefore, from the point of view of the mind, of "non-awareness". It's like standing in front of the sun, I say, "The sun exists," and then turning my back on it, I said, "The sun doesn't exist."

Likewise, awareness – which is our nature – is always present, but conscious recognition by the mind of its presence comes and goes depending on where our attention is.

We realize that we are always aware in relation to something, and the objects become in our minds what causes our being aware. When the object is clear in our mind in its thought-form or emotion or sensation, then we'll say that we are aware and present; when our attention wanders seemingly objectless and aimless, then we'll say that we are unaware and absent. Reality is exactly the opposite: awareness is always present, like the air we breathe, and sometimes, through the reflection of the object and our attention to that object, we recognize the presence of awareness, sometimes not. Just as sometimes we notice that we are breathing and sometimes not. Breathing does not disappear, it is always there, but its mental recognition comes and goes.

Being unaware is impossible, awareness is to us like moisture to water or hardness to a diamond. The presumption of ignorance and unawareness is precisely that, a presumption, a concept, a belief imprinted in our mental program, a part of the software that is called conditioning.

Existentially it is a lie and has no meaning or value other than what YOU give it. The realization that is needed can be enclosed in the transition from the statement "I am aware" to the direct experience "I am awareness".

Five minutes (4)

1:44 p.m.

Who is in?

Outside it has recently rained and there is some moisture in the air and an almost heaviness that does not correspond to inside. Inside I feel light, euphoric, in movement... I'm here and I'm here to stay, not right away but soon... the thought goes quickly towards a future that is not in here... pause, coming back to me, eyes closing for a moment... I start again and the birds outside accompany me, how beautiful!... a sigh of, I don't know exactly what, relief? gratitude? Joy of not knowing? The Koan takes me for a walk without direction or need to understand, without project or... I miss the word and I like this sense of incomprehensible fragility.

I look at the weather... I can hear cars passing by... I'm stable inside... the buttocks not only resting but almost sunk in the chair...

1:50 p.m.

Inquiry (4)

1. Explore the theme of curiosity. What's your relationship to curiosity in your life? Will you allow yourself to be curious? And what relationship do you recognize in yourself between curiosity and creativity?

2. In which areas of your life do you recognize you are creative, and in which areas don't you? What limits your creativity?

3. Explore now the theme of space and your associations with it. Observe how the perception of space changes depending on your mood, your mental and emotional condition; what do you notice?

4. Creativity and space, what do you notice in relation to this combination?

5. Explore your understanding and experience of the different types of fear, in your mind, heart, and belly, starting with the one that's most familiar to you. Give yourself time to connect with each of them by feeling that area of the body. Do not be in a hurry and do not look for hasty answers; fear often manifests itself in different forms: fog, confusion, accelerated thinking, tremor, shortness of breath, mental emptiness, etc. Every situation is different and, at the same time, each of us has personal ways of experiencing fear. GIVE YOURSELF PERMISSION AND SUPPORT TO INVESTIGATE AND WELCOME WHAT YOU FIND, WITHOUT JUDGMENT IF POSSIBLE. At the end of the exploration take some notes. Repeat this inquiry when you can; the goal is to enter into a relationship of familiarity with your fears and dissolve denial, resistance and generalization.

6. LIVING WITHOUT FEAR, what happens inside you when you read these words? What does your inner judge say about it? What are the main obstacles you see in front of you and what are the possibilities? How can you actually support yourself to learning to live without fear?

7. What is your understanding of presence? How do you recognize when you're present and when you're not? What are the signs, symptoms, sensations in the body?

8. What happens to you if you think TOTAL INCLUSIVENESS?

Five

$1 = 0 = \infty$, One equals zero equals infinity

Understanding is the only discipline.
Osho, mystic

Understanding; a word of incredible beauty and existential necessity.

Understanding means that all that we are, in all dimensions, facets and capabilities surrenders to the Real and completely welcomes it through the disappearance of any resistance.

A central step in the search for and experience of truth is to understand its paradoxical nature: to affirm and understand that if the truth is not paradoxical it is not truth.

Truth is all there is. There is no exclusion. There is no comparison. There is no ranking. There is no separation and no boundaries. Paradox is by its very nature absolutely inclusive; it expands in all directions and dimensions.

In Zen this understanding is expressed with the formula: one equals zero equals infinity.

This understanding cannot be only intellectual, it needs to be directly experienced: physical, emotional, mental and spiritual. When this experience happens then all our Being responds naturally, recognizing one's true nature.

This understanding can begin with a process of integrating the paradox into oneself and gradually transforming into a dissolution of the subject in paradox/truth, as well as through the opposite path: beginning with the dissolution of the subject in truth, later transforming into the truth dissolving into the subject.

Often this direct experience is represented through the image of the drop dissolving into the ocean, or the ocean dissolving into the drop.

To live in uncertainty is to live in abundance

The whole world is smart and I'm just an idiot.
Lao Tzu, mystic

This may seem to you quite strange: there is a fundamental paradox in existence of which we are very often unaware because our attention is mostly compulsively fixed on seeking security in all its forms.

We keep telling ourselves: "When I am rich, when I have a good job, when I have found the right person, when I am enlightened, then everything will be all right." There is no point in the universe showing us every day, indeed every moment, that certainty is an illusion and that the fundamental law that regulates existence is change; unpredictable and uncontrollable. In economics, social sciences, statistics, science in general, cohorts of individuals try to predict future events, behaviors and trends and, in the face of some temporary foresight success, they delude themselves that they have found certainty.

Real scientists on the other hand know that every point of arrival is just a new starting point and that what they think they know is an infinitesimal slice of mystery in its continuous and indomitable evolution.

The search for security has always been part of human adventure and it is perfectly understandable that in an unpredictable and mysterious world we seek moments of certainty. However, the fact that we organize our lives so we can have these moments of certainty does not mean it is valid to live in the illusion that safety is possible, and that it is enough to want it or to look for it or plan our lives so that one day... when everything is in its place...

Above all, it is castrating and dehumanizing to be blind to the price we pay in the name of certainty, blind to the lies that we must tell ourselves and others; blind to how the search for certainty inevitably narrows the field of possibilities in the present, as we try to lock the future into what we think we can see based on the past. All this, and many more shadows we try to cast all hide behind the hope that "one day"...

The paradox I mentioned earlier is that the more we seek security, the more we are obliged to narrow the scope thus we delude ourselves that we have some form of control over the present and the future, and we are forced to live in scarcity. On the contrary, when we learn not to control the present moment and surrender to its unpredictability, immediately the field of available possibilities opens up immensely and manifests the vastness of Being and its intrinsic abundance. Abundance without qualifications, without pre-established values based on the past, abundance of everything, what we consider good and what we consider bad.

This abundance obliges us to constantly review three essential aspects of our reality and, more specifically, of our ego identity:

Our image of ourselves and our relative image of the world in which we live.
Our concepts about ourselves and what we call reality (just a description we stick to).
Our personal history.

When we learn to live in uncertainty, we live in a universe that has mobile and transparent boundaries; we make plans and projects, but we are not attached to them or worried about whether they happen or not; success and failure disappear along with the fear of living and dying.

Reflections on Support and Devotional Love

Love happens, you know?
Kabir, mystic

1.

The question of support is central to the path of spiritual search, and it is a direct responsibility of any seeker to consciously create an adequate, efficient, functional, flexible and aesthetic supporting environment; one that is an expression of the uniqueness of the one who seeks. This means that if, at the beginning, there is a similar environment for everyone that responds to the fundamental needs of the seeker, as the search advances, refines and becomes personal, thus free from preconceptions, prejudices and the past, the more the supporting environment takes on forms and qualities that reflect the individuality that lies at its core.

The first and fundamental steps with regard to support have to do with learning to give it to oneself and to recognize when we receive it. Then emerges the question of trusting the support we give to ourselves and the support we receive from others. As we start giving support to others too, it is a question of not feeling special because we give it; and then, in the end it's about having the courage to ask for support without expecting others to give it to us and to give it to others without expecting them to receive it or be thankful.

Some signs to recognize when we're learning to support ourselves:

1. We are able to recognize when we are not present and we don't feel guilty about that.
2. The body becomes an anchor in the here/now.
3. We are aware if we have expectations, we are able recognize them and do not change anything.

4. We have an existential, and not just an intellectual, understanding of the relative truth, and this allows us to quickly identify the origin of conflicts.
5. Our attention moves down, towards the roots, and aligns with the force of gravity.
6. Our whole organism manifests a particularly strong density.
7. We hear our voice as we say whatever we say.

2.

Further signs that help us recognize we are learning to support ourselves emerge, and here is the most important: WE LEARN TO ASK OURSELVES QUESTIONS WITHOUT WAITING FOR IMMEDIATE ANSWERS. This indicates to us that our curiosity to know ourselves and the world we live in, our curiosity to open to the living mystery of the here/now both in the subject that experiences it (I) and of the objects that are its manifestation, has become the central engine of our life. We are learning to master the ability to be present and open to the Mystery of Existence that unfolds beyond any possibility of control. When this curiosity manifests itself and begins to flow uninterruptedly in our veins then we begin to know EXPERIENTIALLY two wonderful aspects of reality: devotional love and inner guidance.

3.

What does devotional love have to do with asking questions without waiting for immediate answers? An open exploration of reality, within and without, a willingness to travel in mystery without excluding anything, without grasping to control, without determined positions a priori, without prejudice: this is a central aspect of devotional love, LOVE FOR TRUTH. Passion, surrender, devotion, enchantment for the Truth, now and at all times.

I surrender, I melt, I am enticed, I am invited and supported in this mysterious present by THE LOVE FOR TRUTH and this LOVE FOR TRUTH that is DEVOTIONAL LOVE is powerful, passionate, burns relentlessly, moves the heart and belly and mind and genitals. It is FIRE, not mine, not yours, FIRE, THE EVOLUTIONARY DYNAMISM OF TRUTH that manifests itself through DEVOTIONAL LOVE EMBODIED in me, in you, in all the unlimited forms that truth takes in its manifesting. Absolutely INCLUSIVE love of everything that is.

4.

The technique we use to express and nurture devotional love and invite guidance is that of open inquiry: exploration, asking ourselves questions, turning on with our curiosity the experiential direct understanding of the truth at this time. The word open indicates our availability to the revelation of meaning in any form and direction. WE ARE INCLUSIVE AND UNPREJUDICED: everything that is, is exactly as it is without us rejecting or grasping. In this openness and love for the truth the invitation to guidance is answered. Being manifests itself in each of us embodied through its ability: mirror awareness, pure, simple, immediate.

About a year and a half before leaving the body Osho gave a series of speeches collected in a book titled *The Great Zen Master Ta Hui*. Chapter 24 of the book – has an incredibly significant title: The Inescapable. The whole talk is a jewel of clarity with respect to meditation and in particular addresses a fundamental issue for any spiritual seeker that many do not expect or even try to avoid. Osho reminds us that IN THE SEARCH FOR TRUTH THE HARDEST PART IS NOT RECOGNIZING WHAT IS FALSE, BUT RATHER LEARNING TO BE PRESENT WITH WHAT IS REVEALED, WHAT IS TRUE. If I look at this understanding from the perspective of support, what does it mean to support myself in living the truth that is unveiled from what was false and hid it?

Two central topics:

Habits. Supporting ourselves in truth means RECOGNIZING THE USUAL MECHANISMS THROUGH WHICH WE RECREATE AUTOMATISM AND UNCONSCIOUSNESS IN OUR DAILY LIFE AND ACTING CONCRETELY TO CHANGE THEM. And this is where love for truth, our inclusiveness, and guidance are central parts of support. They help us to stop splitting from our habits by pretending that they do not exist, and instead we see, recognize, understand and welcome them without judgment. In short, the issue clearly becomes not habits in themselves but our unawareness of them. Rejection disappears and habits become obvious and familiar, not compulsive or denied. If we like them, we keep them, and if not, sometimes even with difficulty, we get rid of them.

Integration and actualization. The support that has enabled us to realize the truth by recognizing that what is false needs to adapt to new phases where the question is not only about the realization of the truth but it is also, and significantly, about the integration of our understandings into everyday life and our capacity to act with truth. We are no longer dealing with WHAT THE TRUTH IS since we can recognize it behind the egoic tendency to self-delusion. Now we are dealing with HOW TRUTH REPLACES IN MY ORGANISM THE HABIT OF FALSEHOOD, HOW I DIGEST THE TRUE AND, AGAIN, HOW I TRANSFORM THIS INTEGRATION INTO THE TRUTH THAT ACTS.

5.

Being present, doing inquiry, developing the ability to move attention, focusing on intention, being open to mystery and all the other skills I have described, devotional love... guess what the good, indeed wonderful news about this is? These are all capacities which are INTRINSIC TO OUR NATURE, we do not need to invent or create them. They already exist in each of us, they are qualities of Being and indeed, even better, WE ARE MADE OF THESE QUALITIES AND RESOURCES. They exist as potential that only needs to be awakened. So how do we awaken the dormant potential so that the support of our soul, of our True Nature, is nourished, strengthened and stabilized?

Here two words become fundamental: PRACTICE AND DISCIPLINE.

Yes, I know, the word discipline to many makes the hair rise on the back of the neck, invites rebellion and a nice NO! I don't know about you, but it certainly was like that for me for many years, until I began to feel that discipline. If it was me who chose it, if it was me who defined its times, quality, intensity, etc... Something began to change when I realized that MY discipline SUPPORTED ME AND MY SOUL. And then one day I heard Osho say that the root of the word discipline is disciple, and everything changed, radically.

There is no "Discipline", there IS YOUR DISCIPLINE, YOUR WILL AND YOUR ABILITY TO PRACTICE WHAT YOU NEED AND HELPS TO CREATE A NOURISHING GROUND FOR THE SEEDS OF YOUR POTENTIAL. So, practice is the search for YOUR DISCIPLINE, it is the ABSOLUTELY PERSONAL journey through which you discover HOW to be present, HOW to make inquiry, HOW to feel love, HOW to be open to mystery. There is no abstractly right way, existence is not so miserable as to give limits to the manifestation of the spirit: there are infinite possibilities in infinite combinations.

6.

"The supporting environment" is defined in psychology as the environment in which the baby finds itself growing especially in the first year: nine months in the mother's belly and another three or four of what is called "symbiotic phase" – the mother's arms and body, the cradle, the room where there is the cradle, etc. It is clear that we do not choose the conditions of this environment and, I imagine, it is also intuitively clear how those conditions determine the original imprint of our relationship with support in subsequent years.

Understanding, nourishment, conscious participation in the creation of an adequate, stable, dynamic, alive, brilliant, personal, intimate, unique supporting environment is probably the most obvious and rewarding result of our learning to support ourselves, and, for the spiritual seeker, a fundamental necessity.

What was once (as children) given from the outside now manifests itself as an overflow from within the presence of Being. This conscious supportive environment has the characteristics I wrote about earlier (and more...): devotional love, guidance, inclusiveness, discipline, curiosity, integration skills, and so on. Understanding the theme of support is absolutely fundamental for any seeker of truth, for anyone who has a sincere yearning to be and know themselves: Support for our Being, for our True Nature is one of the things, perhaps the thing, that was most lacking in childhood for many – sometimes, unfortunately, together with love. For others, there has been support in some ways but not in others, and this has created confusion and made us unbalanced, lacking.

When the question WHO AM I? begins to agitate inside then the question of material, emotional, mental and above all spiritual support becomes inevitable. In my life I have been lucky enough to receive a lot of support, in family, in sport, among my companions in the political struggle in youth, by my martial arts masters, by the women I loved and love, by friends met on the way, by spiritual teachers, by my master and love Osho, by his commune, by dogs, cats and parrots. In some way, wherever I turned, whatever path or adventure I took, whatever dark side I needed to unveil, I found support, contact, mirror, guidance; I also see with absolute clarity that there was in me a fertile ground of support for myself that attracted, received and honored everything that was offered to me from the outside and how Spirit was already and always in action in the here/now.

What I've tried to paint at times very broadly is an understanding and a set of directions that can be helpful to informing how to create a conscious supporting environment for yourself and the people around you. This supportive environment is infused mainly with two essential qualities, what is called White Essence or Essential Will: intention, stable presence, support, commitment, solidity; and the Golden Essence: curiosity, joy, merging, devotion, lightness, playfulness. When you're immersed in the Essential Supporting Environment, you're full, overflowing, radiant with white and gold light. You're supportive and supported. Consciously and abundantly.

The fine line between Narcissism and wanting attention

Laughter is the first evidence of freedom.
R. Castellanos, poet

When I speak with people, I have noticed that nearly everybody thinks of Narcissism as a compulsive love affair with one's own image and therefore an even more compulsive need to get positive reflection from outside.

Without any doubt this is the most obvious and visible aspect of narcissism, and as such it is understandable that it is categorized as a personality disorder.

However, when I look behind the most obvious effects, and search for the spiritual roots of narcissism I see something much more fundamental, and that is the INCAPACITY, UNWILLINGNESS OR UTTER REJECTION OF GOING INSIDE. For most people it seems to be impossible to conceive that instead of looking out one could look in to understand oneself and the world.

So, in this sense narcissism affects pretty much every person and every society.

We are taught, conditioned, forced, brutalized so that we look out, become narcissistic and forget ourselves.

As we lose the sense of our intrinsic value we search externally.

As we lose the connection with our uniqueness, we try to be special in every possible way, open and hidden.

As we lose the sense of being love we search for it in the eyes and arms of others.

As we lose the clarity of awareness and inner guidance, we substitute it with knowledge and rules given by others.

And so on...

The whole society is based on narcissism and nurtures it in every possible way.

And the economic aspect is a primary component of it through one of the fundamental distortions: "The more I HAVE, the more I AM."

Looking at narcissism spiritually means to recognize that we are all narcissistic in different degrees and ways, and to recognize how this narcissism keeps us chained to survival, self-image and the need to belong to a limited tribe.

Now, compulsively wanting attention can certainly be the manifestation of a personality disorder. However, for the majority of people it has nothing to do with that.

In fact, wanting attention carries in itself a mostly unconscious desire for nourishment that is completely natural and even profoundly intelligent.

As living organisms, we instinctively know that ATTENTION IS ENERGY and that we exist as electromagnetic fields that continuously and inevitably relate with the real in a vital network of interdependency.

Wanting attention is not bad or a problem, it is a natural

instinct. The issue with it is THAT WE ARE MOSTLY NOT CONSCIOUS OF IT AND NOT HONEST ABOUT IT.

So please, recognize that everything that grows, grows better when it receives attention. That attention is energy which feeds our energy fields and is at the core of existing in the form. All children know that and try to get all the attention they can, positive if possible and negative otherwise: anything but indifference.

And, even though we like to pretend otherwise in most cases, we all keep wanting attention. So, COME OUT! Let's be honest and simple with this, and give ourselves permission to feel our need and throw away guilt, shame, self-deception.

Narcissism and Compassion

Humility is the recognition of the truth about oneself.
Dabeet in *Children of the Fleet* by O.S. Card

Narcissism from a spiritual point of view is one of the most common phenomena in humanity as it implies the compulsive looking outside to know oneself and the world, rather than looking in.

This compulsive looking out makes us impotent as we separate from our inner resources and look for solutions, approval, definition, identity externally. It also keeps nurturing an inner shakiness and fear. What if people do not like me? Approve of me? Recognize me? What if people see that I am fake? That I am pretending? And so on.

Therefore, narcissism is a core tension that characterizes any personality in its forgetfulness of True Nature.

What does it have to do with Compassion? What is the connection between these two?

At first sight these two seem very improbable partners and yet?

First, here is a basic definition of Compassion...

COMPASSION IS THE CAPACITY AND WILLINGNESS TO LET YOURSELF BE.

Compassion is therefore an all-inclusive sense of oneself that extends naturally and spontaneously to all there is.

Compassion is I AM ALL THAT I AM AND EVERYTHING IS ALL THAT IT IS, and I have the capacity and the intelligence to let myself be in all that I am, and everything be as it is in any present moment. There is no rejection of anything that appears moment to moment and there is no hope for anything different.

The fundamental movement of "rejection and hope" that defines the activity in the mind is realized in its suchness and integrated. Not judged, not evaluated, not pushed away or attached to, but simply recognized and included like the barking of a dog or the sound of a car outside the window, the rain falling or the clouds moving, the breath coming in and going out, the heart beating. We let ourselves be in every aspect of our existing.

Compassion is therefore the conscious dropping of the pressure of becoming in the realization that Being and Becoming are inextricably intertwined and interdependent. As Buddha says: Nirvana is Samsara and Samsara is Nirvana.

Then compassion is the door that opens up into the Real within and without, and establishes a fundamental ground of understanding and realizing what is in its suchness.

As the artificial boundary between the Inner and the Outer fades away, so does narcissism, and the pressure of wanting to be special dissolves into the simple and direct experience that each sentient being and everything is already special and incomparable in its uniqueness.

Five minutes (5)

11:22 a.m.

I came back home at Bondi after my two-week retreat in the

north of NSW where I went to jump-start writing this book. I am sitting at my desk, and I feel at home, in front of the desktop and with a large keyboard... my fingers go fast and secure, I am comfortable and happy to be here... the external noises are familiar and very different from those of the past days, and I feel inside the difference with a sense of curiosity which is an elongation of the spine and also of the ears upwards like an animal... I have very good ears, sensitive and mobile and I am proud of it... they help me a lot to get to know the world outside and also to feel inside... yes, I listen with other ears to the sounds inside that are the deepest sources of my perception, and as I write it, I recognize it... I look at the watch and I have a few more seconds and I like that here I can write faster, and this pleasure manifests itself as a kind and light smile on the lips...

11:27 a.m.

Inquiry (5)

1. Explore your quest for certainty in your life. How does it manifest itself? How do you recognize it? What are the most familiar symptoms that make you realize that certainty is what you are looking for? How do you experience it in the body? Explore without prejudice and, above all, with kindness towards yourself.

2. The theme of abundance: your ideas, concepts, associations with this word... and your reactions when you think about it. Are you expanding? Do you contract? Are you in confusion? What are the main reactions you notice?

3. Explore support. Did you feel support in your family when you grew up? What was supported and what was not? There were conditions for you to be given support: If you are... Do... then... Is it possible, acceptable for you to ask for support? And receive it?

4. In which areas of your life do you feel that you are able

to support yourself and in which do you feel weak or incapable?

5. Explore your availability and capacity to support others. Do you do it out of duty? Do you feel you're free or not? Does it weigh on you? Does it give you joy? What moves inside you when you do this investigation?

6. In light of the spiritual understanding of narcissism: what reflections can you make about your willingness and ability to go inside?

7. Is it acceptable to want attention? What kind of attitude do you have about this? How does your seeking attention manifest itself, openly or sideways? Observe the physical reactions and your inner atmosphere as you explore.

8. Letting yourself be: what does it mean to you? What resonates in this vision of compassion? Is it clear to you that letting yourself be is the necessary condition to letting others be?

9. The question of intention is central to all seeking and practice. Explore your understanding of it and the ways in which intention or lack of it manifests itself in your life. How do you recognize when the intention is clear and powerful, or shaky and inaccurate? What relationship do you see between intention and will?

10. The understanding of Karma brings to light the question of personal responsibility for the messages we put in the field. What do you think? Do you feel reactive and resistant about it? How can you support yourself in the awareness of your responsibility?

Six

Intention, Will and Karma

One day a student from Chicago came to the Providence Zen Center and asked Seung Sahn Soen-sa, "What is Zen?" Soen-sa held his Zen stick above his head and said, "Do you understand?" The student said, "I don't know."
Soen-sa said, "This don't know mind is you. Zen is understanding yourself."
Stephen Mitchell, author

1.

In Martial Arts, Chinese Medicine and many mystical schools, a principle is set out that can help enormously in our understanding of how we unknowingly but effectively support the convulsive activity of thought. This principle can also help in how to stop doing so: "Attention leads Awareness, Awareness leads Energy." This simply means that when we move our attention, that tends to align our awareness, and where awareness goes that tends to move our energy. This dynamic occurs in most cases unconsciously and therefore without us noticing and apparently occurs accidentally. What makes alignment conscious and voluntary is the practice of presence. If I am present, I can shift my attention to will and therefore my awareness and energy.

The excess energy, which almost everyone has in their head, comes from a compulsive excess of attention to the thought process. All meditations therefore emphasize shifting our attention to the body: to breathing, to the way we walk, to the way we look, hear, feel or touch. The physical object of our attention does not matter: the simple act of moving it from thought/imagination to physical sensations inevitably redirects our awareness and energy flows.

When our attention is turned to emptiness, then we experience complete freedom and fluidity, there is no object or experience that occupies our awareness and controls energy. An example: imagine being in a very crowded street or on the subway at rush hour: if you don't try to control it, the body naturally knows how to move in the crowd avoiding obstacles and finding its own rhythm, and knows how to do it effortlessly. The attention is naturally and spontaneously focused on the space between the moving physical masses, awareness follows and adapts the movement of the body and the energy necessary to move it. If you try to focus attention on an external object – for example another person – or an internal object – such as a thought or emotion – you'll sooner or later clash with someone or something, or have to control the energy, creating tension in the system. Every thought needs your attention, and as soon as it has that, it will grab your awareness and suck your energy, becoming a problem and obstacle. The Ego loves obstacles and problems, they are the building blocks of its existence. Leave thoughts at the edges of your attention.

2.

Intention is the result of congruence and alignment on a point (an idea, an action, a feeling, a vision, a sensation, a desire, an understanding, etc.) of attention, awareness and energy. The more we learn to consciously direct and shift our attention, the easier it is for awareness and energy to align naturally. This is the basis of the attention to breath in Vipassana meditation; to the body position in the Zazen; to walk consciously; to fast breathing in the first phase and stillness in third phase of Osho's dynamic meditation; to observe the flame of the candle in Tratak Meditation: the purpose is, SINGLEPOINTEDNESS! Totality of focus on one point.

There are two basic ways to achieve this totality of concentration: one is exclusive and therefore relies on excluding anything other than what you focus on, and this is the most common and generally taught mode in schools etc. where "the field of awareness is reduced". It's like using a telephoto lens in a camera (100mm up). This is also the most widespread scientific mode: control of the environment and variables.

The other is inclusive which means that any input which manifests itself in awareness is included, and there is no effort to limit the field but a progressive rapprochement and contact with the object of our attention "within an open field". It's like using a wide angle in photography (25mm down...).

The fundamental egoic reality is separation and therefore exclusion, hierarchy, comparison, and ego – which is fundamentally fragmented, isolated, divided, contradictory, confusing – has an inherent difficulty in focusing attention by keeping the field open if not for very limited periods and, in most cases, compulsively tends towards exclusion and narrow focus in the illusion that this attitude makes the goal clearer and allows for greater control over the result. Thus, the expression of egoic intention tends to be exclusive and reductive with respect to reality and is based on a perception of the universe as fundamentally dualistic. Inevitably it coincides with effort, tension and rigidity.

The essential intention (the one that embodies the presence and contact with the authentic Self and the quality of Essential Will) is the natural manifestation of the presence and non-separation of the individual and the reality in which they live, and is therefore the conscious and natural ability to focus all energy, awareness and attention on a point in the continuous and dynamic change of the present moment without excluding anything.

Egoic intention is a creative mode of personality based on "doing" to bend the world to personal will; essential intention is an expression of individual/universal creativity in their coincidence, and concerns "being". Both are aspects of the creative process but egoic intention has an extremely limited power because it is based on a fragmentary and unstable alignment of attention/awareness/energy while the true intention – natural and conscious alignment of attention/awareness/energy – expresses the power of the individual surrendered to all that is and in resonance with it.

3.

The transition from egoic to essential intention is both an event and a process. The event coincides with the radical and complete understanding – not only intellectual but also in the heart and belly – of the fundamental illusion in which the personality lives regarding the relationship between individual will and cosmic will. Personality continually tries to bend reality to its fantasy of greatness and narcissism by doing everything to impose, determine and manipulate external reality to respond to its desire; rarely does this occur. In the absolute majority of cases there is failure and frustration which, in the absence of understanding, leads to further effort and hard determination, up to fanaticism and the most abject fundamentalism. The process has to do with integrating radical understanding into everyday life by opening us to feeling the deep pain generated by the separation between individual will and the will of existence, as well as our yearning for unity and union; it also has to do with the actualization of this radical understanding in a concrete way by revealing and letting go of our grandiose/miserable attitude day after day, situation after situation, relationship after relationship.

Radical understanding opens the door to a paradox: the contemporary and complementary manifesting of a recovery of personal power parallel to an ever deeper surrender to what is: power = openness, strength = vulnerability, will = surrender. The recognition of the fundamental impotence of my efforts, the isolation and frustration that it creates, the egoic swing "from the stars to the stables" open the door to a deep and long-hidden pain regarding our belonging to this universe and our place in it, and also accelerates the recognition of karmic dynamics: WHAT I PUT IN THE FIELD RETURNS TO ME, and the need to take responsibility for what I put in the field. THERE IS NO ROOM FOR SELF-PITY!

How do I know if the shift from egoic to essential intention is happening? The tendency to effort and stubbornness that indicate egoic intention tends to decrease while clearly increasing a sense of contentment and flowing into everyday life as an effect of the alignment of the individual will with that of existence along with many other pleasant surprises.

4.

KARMA: The universe works like an ecosystem, literally. What you put in it is returned as it happens with the echo. If I put fear, I get back fear; if I put suffering, I get back suffering; if I put joy, I get back joy; if I put desire, I get back desire; if I put beauty, I get back beauty; if I put abundance, I get back abundance... The timings of the echo are unpredictable, but the return is certain, in a continuous recreating of a dynamic equilibrium. The more conscious the intention and clear the alignment of attention, awareness and energy, the clearer the message I put in the field and the more powerful and immediate the response of the ecosystem.

In Zen, the general and more basic state of egoic unconsciousness is called "attachment to name and form" and corresponds to what is called KARMA I. The one who lives attached to the name and form (and does not know it...) does not experience reality but only a description of reality made of names and forms that are assumed as real. So, they think that calling a shoe a shoe says something about the object itself, talking about love or truth means knowing something about one or the other; this one never asks: "If I change the name and call the shoe smoke or fish, will it change my direct experience (not symbolic...) of the object?" The symbols of language have taken the place of the real. So, I call fear or anxiety an experience that I live and lock into that name something that I have no real understanding and knowledge of, and I think I know why I named it that name. In this situation of fundamental unconsciousness, I create Karma by moving like an elephant in a crystal store, but without animal innocence. I am childish, narcissistic and fundamentally convinced that I am the victim of an existence from which I feel separated. Not only do I not recognize karmic law, but I stubbornly place responsibility for what happens to me outside of me. At the same time, I try in every way to convince myself that I am able to condition the result of my actions. In this state of fragmentation and unconsciousness the message I put in the field is weak, incomplete, confused; intention is like a flame that trembles continuously and risks dying out.

Only the presence and authenticity of the true Self can stabilize the flame, make it bright and constant; only responsible intention (which knows how to respond to the present moment instead of re/act through the past...) has the ability to put in the field clear messages that manifest the intersection of individual will and that of existence. These messages arise spontaneously from the direct experience (not mediated by name and form) of reality. Karma then is not something that happens to us and dominates our humanity, but an aspect of the dynamic movement of cosmic consciousness that manifests itself as a conscious interaction between the individual and the Absolute, God, Primary Awareness, Spirit.

Causality and the law of attraction

Experience is not what happens to you, it's what you do with what happens to you.
Aldous Huxley

1.

Each effect has a cause, and vice versa. If I want to have a certain effect, I have to act on the possible causes. Fundamental Socratic intuition became a law of science with Newton in the Third Law of Movement: "Every action corresponds to an equal and contrary reaction." And it is often on the basis of this intuition that we have made law which we strive to create the conditions for, to determine the path of, to influence the result, to explain ourselves through the past, to justify something by looking for possible causes. It can certainly be useful, and it is, enormously, in scientific advances and in the material world, but are we sure that this "law" has not become part of our prison? One of the symptoms of this prison is the obsession with seeking the why of things, the reasons for my feeling or my acting in a certain way; if I just understand why this or that happens, if only I could define the cause of my suffering, if only I could understand the reason why she left me, why I'm not successful, why I can't manifest wealth or the work I want...

The need to find a WHY is an integral part of the attachment to the name and form and therefore to a description of reality made of symbols assumed to be true. The search for why tends to narrow the field of exploration by limiting the real to understandable and definable relationships, and therefore to concepts, values and beliefs that fall within a particular description of the world in which I exist. The mystery disappears, freedom disappears, the unpredictable immensity of the present moment disappears, fundamental union and unity disappear with all that is here. Now.

The search for meaning: "This is the case because this happened, and I know how to define it... ah! now I can breathe!" IT'S PURE ILLUSION. How often in your affective, sentimental life, in spirit, heart, belly, beauty, moments of creativity and passion, expressive explosions, meditation, sexuality and pleasure, prayer, play, running in the rain or swimming in the current, in combat while the sword falls, or with the brush in hand... how often did you really need to know why? Know the (alleged) cause? Did you need linear logic and cause-and-effect philosophical determinism?

If you want to start LIVING life and not suffer it, if you want to be a responsive, efficient and creative part of Karma you can only throw yourself into the mystery of this moment and feel it by letting a much deeper intelligence find connection and expression, free from "name and form", free from identification with an "I" defined and determined by personal history.

2.

Simply put, the law of attraction says that we attract into our lives what we put our dominant thoughts on, our dominant emotions, our dominant beliefs – and all these things are obviously more or less dense forms of vibrational fields. THIS ATTRACTION TAKES PLACE BASICALLY UNCONSCIOUSLY, and being almost always an expression of an egoistic intention that, as seen above, is fragmented, confused, contradictory and above all separated from the field and unable to recognize the moving forces that determine what is happening (attachment to name and form, attachment to cause/effect etc.) has a near-zero chance of succeeding and attracting ONLY what it wants.

Example: I want abundance and I try in every way to create a vibrational field that attracts abundance but – of course there is a "but" here – if I am not aware of the negative beliefs that can exist in my unconscious with respect to abundance such as: "be careful not to have too much because others become jealous"; if I do not recognize that abundance concerns everything without distinction and therefore also abundance of anger, jealousy, fear, etc. and "I hope" only in the abundance of what I like; if I want plenty of recognition and do not include the possibility of an abundance of criticism then these information/vibrations are also inevitably entered into the field. IT SEEMS OBVIOUS

TO ME THAT I EXIST IN AN ENERGY FIELD BASED ON JUDGMENT AND SEPARATION, PREFERENCES AND CONDITIONS! AND, IN YOUR OPINION, DOES EXISTENCE RESPOND TO SOMETHING SO TINY AND PETTY? Yes! It responds by sending back separation, confusion, frustration, disregarded desires, name and form... karmic return pure and simple. This idea that the little ego at the core of personality has the ability to influence or even determine at his own will the response of the cosmic energy field is typical of the delusion of grandiosity, and only reinforces narcissism and that attitude of "I have the right to have what I want" that is increasingly typical of our society and which, unfortunately, I must admit has been strongly characteristic of the generation of baby boomers; my generation.

Awakening, awareness conscious of itself

Be formless, shapeless, like water.
Bruce Lee, martial arts master

1.

For years and years I have lived, like the absolute majority of humanity, fixed on the objects. My awareness existed as an uninterrupted stream of things that appeared and quickly disappeared invariably replaced by other things. This is the "normal" and widespread human condition, and we take it for granted. Yet, I had experienced, like probably many others, moments of deep joy, great excitement, ecstatic moments when something magical had taken over me. It was as if sometimes I jumped over a ditch and found myself in a parallel reality where my attention was not chained to things. When I say "things", I don't just mean physical objects, I also mean the "things" inside, the physical sensations, the emotions, the feelings, the thoughts, the perceptions, the images. Normally it was as if every object

I was aware of had an inherent ability to fully occupy my attention, at least for a moment, excluding everything else. It was a kind of glue, an energy elastic that caught my attention, completely and inexorably. And then, at some point I started to notice that there were times when this wasn't happening and my attention was non-fixated but, how to say this? Open, free, not caught, and how in those moments my inner atmosphere was radically different. A veil of melancholy that I knew well, at least since I was five, six years old, was lifting then.

2.

Playing basketball, making love, diving into the sea, in martial arts, in clashes with the police in the years of my political militancy in Italy, in front of a dazzling sunset... and on many and many other occasions... yes, because I found out later that there were many occasions when my attention was free from the objects of experience.

When I met Osho, he talked about these things and hearing him say them was both hilarious and frustrating, pure joy and "when will it be my time?", "will I ever make it?" to be free from the slavery of objects?

Viscerally I knew, without any evidence, that the retreat called Satori could be where I would find answers to those questions and, in the early 1990s, when I had been living permanently in Pune for a couple of years, I managed to organize a Satori Retreat in Osho's ashram facilitated by Sudha and Ganga as part of the program of the School for Centering and Zen Martial Arts. I felt that participating in this retreat could start a revolution within me, be a challenge that I could not escape, an opportunity to fully immerse myself in the question that I had been carrying for years: Who am I? That was my first Koan.

3.

Three days have passed. I have inquired, meditated, sweated, tried in every way to enter the Koan, to let go of all my ideas, to observe my prison and the objects that populate it, not to hold anything back, not to hide, to show up, to let go of the attachment to knowledge, to go beyond the boundaries of my personality, to lift every stone in the way, to strive to achieve something of which I have only a vague and uncertain understanding. My intention is clear and not wobbly, and something opens up briefly and then closes. Every time this happens the flame of my intention becomes stronger.

It's mid-morning meditation time and this time it's Nataraj where we completely let go in dancing. I close my eyes and let my body follow the music and adapt to the rhythm, and everything slows down, every note is in the foot that touches the floor, in the hand that moves the air, in the breath that fills me and abandons me, in the beauty of not knowing what will be of me in the next moment. Effort disappears leaving the body, mind and soul are free to be, there is no project, expectation, future, there is only a luminous intention that absorbs everything and gives itself without grasping and holding anything. At some point a sort of energy shock goes through me, and in a flash, I simply recognize that I exist. I EXIST!

I simply and directly exist, regardless of what I do, what I think or feel, regardless of my body and the objects around me. I exist and I know I exist. I am. And there's only light. I am only light.

4.

The world is transfigured around me. Time has changed as well as the light and every single shape; everything appears and disappears in consciousness without leaving a trace while I stay. I see that I am staying, or at least I have this impression for a while; objects, things, are no longer such but evanescent transient forms, the glue is no longer there, the elastic of desire and identification has broken and there is a sense of vastness and spaciousness that throbs with contentment and tranquility.

For the first time I finally understand the meaning of my name, Avikal, quiet. And for the first time in two and a half days even the body no longer holds back and crouched on an Indian toilet I have a kind of orgasm! And I laugh at this, and I smile, and I feel a little dumb, and free... in every sense.

When I go back to the mattress and to asking myself the Koan: Who am I? Who am I? the joy of not knowing overwhelms me, envelops me, possesses me, throws me into the mouth of the present moment with the intensity and bliss of a divine lover. At this invitation I surrender in fullness and humility, and also I AM disappears. There is no longer a subject, there is no me, there is only Being, pure presence that is awareness. Liberation. I look inside and I'm not, I can't find myself. I realize it's Being that's looking through my eyes.

5.

At the end of the retreat, I picked up my things and started slow and happy towards the center of the Commune. After a few steps I met a friend, working like me in the School for Centering, who with a look between the curious and the suspicious asked me: "I heard that you got enlightened, did you?" "I don't know if I'm enlightened," I answered smiling, "I certainly know I am."

6.

When I look back to those days, at that moment, I see how all my past, all the periods of darkness and despair, all the challenges and those that seemed mistakes and missteps, were the steps that prepared me, that made me that young man who came to that room, full of passion and commitment, willing to do anything to find himself. Every event, everything prepared me for disappearing. I bow to life and its mysterious unfolding.

Completeness

Absolute perfection is here and now, not in some future, near or far.
The secret is in action – here and now.
It is your behavior that blinds you to yourself.
Disregard whatever you think yourself to be and act as if you were absolutely perfect
– whatever your idea of perfection may be.
All you need is courage.
Nisargadatta Maharaj, mystic

Right now, exactly right now, stop and let your attention open to the awareness of your experience.

Let your attention move freely without choosing what you are aware of. What happens to you in the body? What thoughts come to you? If there are emotions, let go of the internal pressure to define what happens to you, to give names, to associate concepts, to box: this is this, this is that, this is something else and so on, let awareness be open to what's there, BEFORE defining it. Notice what happens in the body while, a little at a time, you let every tension melt, let it fall down to the floor, let go of your shoulders, let go of your buttocks and belly, let go of your forehead and jaws, let go of your eyes and do not look, "see"… Seeing is receptive, the eyes are open without focusing on anything, like two windows they receive the view, everything there is without excluding anything, without avoiding, without even attaching a name, a label, to what you see. Let go of every label, stop cataloguing your experience as it happens, imagine you've forgotten the names you normally give to things, events, what happens. Experience is an A PRIORI compared to the definition we give. The experience takes place and THEN we catalogue it. The label, the name we affix to what we hear, see, touch, taste, smell, perceive, think, imagine, comes AFTER the experience itself and, in some way, limits it and locks it in words that are basically based on descriptions of the reality of the past.

Try to feel what happens in your body if you let go of familiar descriptions; when feeling what you feel is not immediately imprisoned in the words that define it.

Feel how the world seems to expand, lose consistency and definition and, at the same time, how everything becomes more alive and vivid, bright and brilliant... no names! Nothing that locks up what's here right now. Inside and out, they disappear along with the concepts that make them look real. The hand that writes is not HAND, it is absolutely what it is and works how it works, feels how it feels, is free to be and freed from having to be...

The whole universe exists, and us with it, regardless of the names we give, the labels with which we try to assert our dominion over the Real.

You're already complete.

The cosmos is already complete.

This moment is already complete.

Beyond separation: coming to the point

Man is not as complex as he often thinks he is (with a glimmering of satisfaction). He is complex in the sense that a tin of worms is complex. To the observer it is just a tin of worms. What the tin of worms is doing might be complex to the worms, but the observer can tell without looking that they are wriggling and squiggling, like a tin of worms.

Barry Long, mystic

1.

There are two basic ways to go beyond the hypnosis of a separation-based description:

1. Remember a little more every day that as we stick to the hypnosis of a description, that induces a sense of separation. This happens in the horizontal time/space dimension.
2. "Realize" that without attachment both, hypnosis and description, exist within an infinite number of possibilities in the here/now. This happens in the vertical dimension of the eternal present.

The first way is the slow and progressive one that builds on itself step by step until the realization event. This path is the one most traveled by spiritual seekers, more familiar and of which more has been said and written. It is also the one where the terror of the destructuring of defence and survival structures (personality) and its center (egoic identity) is most manageable both in its intensity and quality. The way of "self-remembering" is the way of "practice". It is the path that requires discipline, dedication, commitment, and that also involves many moments of frustration, fall, dismay, despair, valleys, peaks, ecstasy, blessings, connection, intimacy. It is also the way where you can share your experience even if by approximation.

On this path the frozen drop gradually recognizes itself as part of the ocean, witnesses the dissolution of boundaries and their reforming, until they become transparent. The drop melts every day a little, and the surrender to True Nature takes place gradually even if sometimes with sudden and powerful jumps.

2.

In this melting of personality structure, the most powerful and also the most terrifying phenomenon is the opening of Space. I am literally saying that our perception of space both inner and outer changes, sometimes in a sudden and radical way. The Yaqui shaman Don Juan says that, "The world collapses."

When structures made frozen and rigid from years and

years of identification and attachment begin even for a few moments to melt, a central quality to True Nature that is Space manifests itself and this experience brings simultaneously relief, excitement, expansion, beauty as well as a sense of terror. This terror has two characteristic elements: on the one hand it is the telluric shock of the collapse of old defence and survival structures; on the other it is the sudden tsunami of Being that appears inside, outside, everywhere and puts us in front of a reality that we have never seen with such crystal-clear clarity and power. Also, a fundamental belief of personality: that emptiness is negative, the lack of something suddenly explodes in our faces without mediations.

3.

The courage to ask ourselves, "What do I miss?" is the step that allows us to go beyond the terror of the dissolution of personality structures. This is a question "forbidden" by the inner judge because it inevitably exposes the control that locks us in the past and the fundamental scarcity and isolation of egoic identity. This question in fact connects us and opens up what we perceive as energy; physical and emotional holes that we have been carrying with us since time immemorial (in fact from the first months of childhood: lack of love, attention, contact, value, etc.). We realize that we are a colander that continually efforts to APPEAR intact, and this is the fundamental paranoia of the mask that we wear: "What if they realize what I really am?" In avoiding the question "What am I missing?", not only do I unknowingly align myself with the domination of the inner judge, but I also remain disconnected with the repressed material thrown down into the unconscious that, as is its nature, continues to boil trying to come to the surface and to awareness. Sexuality, freedom, authenticity, pleasure, intelligence, satisfaction, passion, recognition, value... there are many hidden treasures that we constantly renounce in the name of the past and cowardice in not facing terror. But why then should it be so terrible TO BE WHO YOU REALLY ARE?

4.

What few understand, or want to understand because it hurts, or only understand intellectually, which is not to understand at all, is that personality is a "doing": an occupying of awareness – which is pure space, intrinsically empty – with the objects of conditioning.

These objects are beliefs, judgments, opinions, values, definitions, etc. that are all "resistances" to emptiness.

This resistance we "make", is suffering.

And this hypnosis of "making" suffering manifests itself in our language in phrases such as: "making love", as if loving could ever be reduced to a "making". We are so powerful that we create our suffering every moment through continuous and stubborn identification with "I am the doer", and this also shows us the high road: surrender and stop doing. For this reason, the spiritual path is fundamentally a "negative way" (in Sanskrit neti neti = neither this nor that), a removing of the obstacles that we continually create, an end to resisting, to defending the past, to occupying the void with the petty objects of MY personal history.

5.

When we begin to ask ourselves, "What do I miss?" perhaps everything inside rebels against this question because inevitably it implies vulnerability, recognition of need, negative emptiness, perhaps expectations, old defences that protect us from feeling our fragility and also question "great" spiritual concepts like: there is everything, nothing is missing, there is only perfection and completeness and so on.

But Spirit is not a concept, it is a real feeling, a Being, not a thought or, worse, a belief. This means that all those concepts are an obstacle until they are erased and replaced by direct experience. The question "What do I miss?" disappears on its own when we are immersed every moment in reality without resistance and without preferences because the question is necessary only as long as I think and act to manipulate and control my experience.

Often masters talk about acceptance and certainly this step is necessary, but do you really think that reality changes whether we accept it or not? Reality does not change at all, it is simply WHAT IT IS. It is our attitude that changes, and this change allows us to see aspects of reality previously hidden. At some point even acceptance disappears and simply remains the REALIZATION that everything is simply as it is, and then perhaps the most powerful piece of the spiritual journey begins: SUBMISSION to the real.

In this submission the question disappears completely together with the doer.

And only then is "Great Perfection" not a concept.

6.

When I follow with absolute dedication, with passion and constancy the path that the question "What do I miss?" opens to me, I find myself, step by step, deleting one object after another. I find myself recognizing over time that it is not something I miss, it is not love or joy or success or value or the other... I MISS MYSELF. Of course, that said, it is not difficult to recognize the obviousness of this recognition: I assure you; it is not. It is not at all obvious to feel again the abyss of despair and absolute deficiency that opens up before you when it becomes clear beyond any doubt or attempt at self-deception that no object, no vision, no feeling, no one else can ever fill that void.

Here submission means bowing to the reality of separation from the Self and not looking for replacements.

Here submission means recognizing not intellectually but in the heart, belly and genitals that "coming home" inevitably means recognizing that I AM ALL THAT IS. And all it is, is all that pain and how we've been used to narcotizing ourselves in a thousand ways for years.

One of the paradoxes of remembrance and awakening is that the recognition and experience of the pain of self-separation is also at the same time the onset of the blessing of union and unity with it that is ecstasy.

In the gradual path this paradoxical coincidence rarely manifests itself in final explosions but rather in a continuous and sweet wonderous contentment, and a progressive and growing ability to live at the intersection point of the time/space dimension (the form) and the vertical dimension of the eternal here/now (the absolute).

Five minutes (6)

3:58 p.m.

Who is in?

I close my eyes and wait......... I feel my exhalation, slow and deep......... and the sound of the washing machine in the kitchen......... I breathe in and my chest and belly expand......... it is a pleasure to feel the breath coming out and grabbing my attention, gently, intimately......... sounds......... voices of children, birds, a car going by......... I notice the light of the new lamp on my desk......... the index finger of the right hand beats on the key......... it has stopped......... I resume writing and listening; it is interesting to give attention to both these things at the same time, noticing that they happen synchronically yet as in two different dimensions, and as I also add what happens outside and is perceived inside, the world widens and includes.

4:03 p.m.

Inquiry (6)

1. Explore your relationship with the why and the wanting to find explanations for the reasons, causes of what happens and for what you do, think, feel...

2. Explore your intention to be present in everyday life, its strength and weakness; in which areas of your life you feel it more clearly and where in the body.

3. Explore the tendency to believe something is missing. Hoping that one day in the future everything will be fine. What effects do these beliefs have in your life? Is there a procrastination? Sabotage? Waiting for salvation?

4. How do you recognize separation in your life? How do you create separation? What investment do you have in continuing to create separation, what do you gain?

5. What are the most obvious effects of the presence of separation in your life?

6. What are your associations with spiritual search? What is your understanding of the search? Who is the seeker? How does seeking manifest itself in your daily life?

7. Explore the attachment to seeking, how it manifests, where it manifests, and with what concrete effects. How does it color your views and opinions? How does it color your relationship?

8. Explore your image as a spiritual seeker and the sense of identity that comes with it.

9. Explore the presence of a sense of superiority over others related to identification with being a seeker.

Seven

Beyond the search

The surest signs of spiritual progress
are a lack of concern about spiritual progress and
an absence of anxiety about liberation.
Ramesh S. Balsekar, mystic

1.

In its very nature, search implies a movement of attention towards something. Whether or not we know what we are looking for is irrelevant in itself and does not change the intrinsic nature of searching. Searching inevitably means a movement of attention from the pure and indefinable presence of the subject (I) to an external object if it is something different from me that I am looking for, or to the subject who has become an object (me) if it is me who I am looking for (or "my" emotions, "my" thoughts etc.). In the search, techniques, maps, resources, paths, are essential tools to support this movement. They often become obstacles, however, at the very moment when we forget – or even deny – that the search itself and the use of any tool for understanding imply and are based on a separation between subject and object: me and the thing I am looking for, me and me.

Any search also has some fundamental expectations in itself: fulfillment, completeness, liberation and certainty. These expectations are transferred by seekers onto the tools they use to search: techniques, maps, resources and paths.

The capacity for self-reflection – the subject (I) becoming the object (me) of a new subject (I) – is undoubtedly the resource that more than any other characterizes humans and is a source of knowledge and evolution. At the same time, it is our most devious prison when it becomes the compulsive habit of self-definition. We do the same with everything, naming everything that exists moment by moment and then objectifying (reifying) nonstop to constantly delude ourselves that we know what it is, that we are present because "we grasp", because we believe we know and understand.

2.

I realize that affirming what I wrote in the previous part can sound strange or even antagonistic to some who sincerely, and through hard work every day seek themselves and are on the spiritual path using various techniques and maps and tools of understanding. It is not my intention to diminish in any way the "work" that we do to grow, to understand, to know, to support us on the way. Indeed, those who know me and work with me know how much I insist on committing day after day to meditating, exploring, cleaning, and letting the old go. At the same time, it is clear to me that all this will not bring what we are looking for, but temporarily it will bring fulfillment, liberation, completeness and certainty. How illusory it is to believe that since precious changes take place now and then, the fundamental lie is somehow undermined that there is a separate self, and that I am the doer.

To give an example, all the search does is recognize, move, tidy up and sometimes change the furniture in our house, but it's clear that as long as I'm searching, it means that I still believe I'm that furniture.

Sometimes identification dissolves, sometimes it disappears altogether but the belief remains that I have to change, improve, have a direction and a purpose. We cannot relax once and for all in the perfect imperfection, uniqueness, completeness and absolute freedom that is our True Nature because as long as we seek, we inevitably move away from it.

If you look closely at the dynamics of desire you will clearly see that the sense of fulfillment, liberation, completeness and certainty which for a short time follows the realization of desire itself has to do with the fact that at least for a moment I AM NOT SEARCHING, I am not going anywhere, I'm only with myself, in my authentic Self, the one that is not seeking, the one that doesn't change, doesn't do, JUST IS.

The task of the search is therefore not realization, because we are "already and always" whole and complete and enlightened; the task of the search is to unlearn the mind and show us our identification with the belief of being the doer.

3.

This understanding cannot be taken lightly or merely with a ritual, yet, it must become the daily spark of our remembering: that we are already complete and unique and that this incarnation, in this body, gives us the concrete opportunity to manifest this uniqueness, this completeness, this enlightenment. That the ego is just fiction, and that as much as it is worth committing to living better with it, that doesn't change the fact that it is a fiction.

The fundamental implication of this internal realignment has to do with our practice: we stop practicing FOR enlightenment and start practicing FROM enlightenment which is who we already are.

Practice is therefore not the search for something that is not here and could take place at a future time, but the concrete manifesting of our awakened consciousness in the here/now.

This fundamental step requires the courage to recognize that WHO IS IN is beyond any description, any understanding, any meaning, and that every tool I use to define myself inevitably implies a reduction of this immensity and mystery. It can be useful to survive but the price is a false certainty.

I DON'T KNOW is one of the keys to "practicing from enlightenment" because false ego identity lives in the self-deception of believing to know, and therefore, when we practice

"I don't know", we are immediately out of identification with the ego; we are again in innocence, and that is a fundamental quality of true nature.

4.

Wake up NOW! There is nothing more selfish and narcissistic than stubbornly continuing to deny one's nature, that of continuing to claim to be the shadow of who we really are: completeness, uniqueness, awareness and love.

Attachment to the search is a disease, and a serious disease! A disease that continues to block millions of human beings who could potentially be ready to take full responsibility for being free and consciously participate in a global rebellion that is the only chance we have left. Using what teaching gives us to survive is an egoic trick; justifying our actions with a "spiritual understanding" is a trick. Finding relief in an alleged spiritual superiority is another trick; thinking of "knowing" is the fundamental trap and withering of the soul.

Every time we look outside, whenever we just find a name, a definition, an excuse to box ourselves and repeat ourselves incessantly... every time we look for someone to blame or someone and something to save us we dispel the precious richness of our humanity and our soul shrivels.

Waking up is not enough!

Nothing can be changed until it is faced.
James Baldwin, author

Let's get clear! Let's throw down from the altars the idols of the past and the idealizations of a spirituality of renunciation, a spirituality stuck on transcendence and far away from daily life. Its time has passed! What is the sense today of sitting under a tree deep into one's own realization while ignoring life, effects, challenges, creativity and evolutionary responsibility?

My experience, my life as an Osho disciple, the very longing of my soul and the passion that I feel inexorably compel me not only to put under scrutiny any idealization of enlightenment (often reductive and dehumanizing) but even more to recognize the optimizing thrust of cosmic consciousness that indissolubly conjugates love and awareness. Where awareness is clear and impersonal presence of the Universal Mind and love, the embodied and very personal manifestation of the Universal Heart.

There are three fundamental points to being fully living in the present and to open up to the natural fulfilment and completeness that our superego continuously denies us.

These three points are the manifestation of the understanding that we are ALREADY free in Being. This intrinsic freedom is also full responsibility for the actualization of our individuality which is the embodiment and higher expression of that freedom.

Conscious evolution as expression of the freedom of a responsible individual implies:

1. Emotional maturity: the conscious letting go of our identification with the inner judge and the child inside.
2. Recognition of one's own shadow: the capacity and willingness to integrate it, purifying it of its own reactivity.
3. Becoming visible and accountable: embodying one's understanding and transformation day after day.

What does it mean to become an adult? What does it mean to mature emotionally?

In my personal experience everything was a big mess until I realized experientially:

1. That there was a fundamental difference between emotions and feelings. That emotions are feelings

locked in time and charged with values, judgments, beliefs, habits and, more than anything else, attachment. Emoting then has nothing to do with the present but is rather a reactivity that repeats acquired patterns.

2. That I had learnt to feel from the feminine (my mother mostly) and therefore I had very little clue about what it meant to feel from the masculine.

3. That the only way to really feel was possible only if I was present in the here/now and I was capable of being present with my feeling experience without immediately attaching a definition or a name to make me feel at ease and in control.

4. Until I stopped fearing women's emotionality and, on the contrary, I started enjoying the immense richness and creativity of their emotional world.

5. Until I discovered that my heart, as it feels, is creating reality in conjunction with the thought-forms generated by the intellect and the actions generated by my guts.

Then to be mature means that I am present, that I am interested in being present and that I am fascinated by being here in this mystery that I am, that the world around is, and allow myself to feel HOW ALL THIS CONTINUOUSLY DISSOLVES ME AND RECOMPOSES ME.

Cleaning up: to know my shadow and purify myself of my reactivity

Most people believe and hope that a final moment exists when everything is done, concluded, when only light is left, when integration is complete and perfect.

This hope prevents them the living of THIS moment and the reality of light/shadow.

A clinical psychiatrist questioned Suzuki Roshi about consciousness. "I don't know anything about consciousness,"

Suzuki said. "I just try to teach my students how to hear the birds sing."

When we let go of the hope of living only as love, light, compassion, and all the other elevated ideals that cloud our perception, then we learn to hear the birds sing.

Let's clean up our home from hope and the illusions of perfection, let's listen with attention to the words of our reactivity and observe its actions, without self-judgment, without putting ourselves down, without manipulation and discover thus the FULLNESS of our humanness.

Showing up

What does it mean to show up and why do it? Uniqueness is the answer, the simple understanding of our uniqueness and the potential to discover it day by day, to consciously embody it, to share it, to contribute to the richness and diversity of Being. It is not mandatory to show up, but it is certainly a celebration of our intelligence, beauty and creativity. Showing up asks us to consciously go beyond our boundaries and to affirm who we really are, regardless of the acceptance and recognition of others. It is not easy, and it is not simple, but it certainly deeply nourishes our confidence in ourselves and our abilities, and brings to the surface our courage to live. And finally, it greatly helps and accelerates the integration of the various shadow materials that slow down or prevent our growth.

Intention and grace

You should do everything – but remember, it is not going to happen simply by your doing. Something happens to you, something unknown; grace descends upon you. Your efforts will make you more receptive to the grace, that's all; but it is not as a direct result of your efforts that grace descends upon you.
Osho, mystic

1.

Once we enter adulthood the question of whether or not to do something, to be or not to be in a certain way is an entirely ALL-INTERNAL matter. Nothing and no one oblige us to survive, to relate, to participate, to live; existence has not placed on us this yoke. Our freedom is, with regard to ourselves, absolute, and within that freedom resides our ability to close relationships that we do not want or to create relationships not based on mediocrity, to change the conditions of our survival, or even to end our lives. The question is not the change itself but rather the whole internal question: "Am I willing to take responsibility for my choices by addressing the consequences?" I repeat, OUR INNER FREEDOM IS ABSOLUTE, there are no excuses, the question is not about the possibilities that are open to us, but about our courage and cowardice, and the habit of staying in the comfort zone. As long as we find, even with noble words and feelings, in other people, in external situations, in ideas and morals, the reasons and justifications of our prison, we are and will remain slaves.

2.

There is a fundamental paradox against which sooner or later the spiritual seeker slams his nose, especially if one has asked with commitment and participation the fundamental questions, "Who is in?", "Who am I?" or other existential questions: What is love? What is truth? What is life? And so on.

The paradox has to do with the RELATIONSHIP BETWEEN INTENTION AND GRACE. Or, if you prefer, the relationship between commitment to practice and discipline on the one hand, and the recognition that direct experience of truth, the REALIZATION OF TRUE NATURE, just happens, is not caused, on the other. This paradox is very often experienced as a conflict, as a difficulty, as an incomprehensible dichotomy: on the one hand the need for a commitment to practice in order to

CAUSE REALIZATION (… is this not for a long time the central motivation for effort in meditation? I want to get enlightened, so I stop suffering?), and on the other hand the frustrating realization that direct experience, the vision of the real, the intuition, the moments of blessing and clarity about who I am and what I am doing here, do not seem to be determined by my will or control but happen on their own.

Here I do not want to get into the heart of this APPARENT conflict; I just want to point that maybe it is the assumption from which we start that is wrong. Perhaps it is the idea that there is or should be a relationship between intention and grace that already puts us on the wrong track. What if the relationship does not exist (relationship occurs between two distinct parts)? What if intention (of the individual) and grace (cosmic intention) were only aspects of a single phenomenon? What if the realization is not OF THE INDIVIDUAL but THROUGH THE INDIVIDUAL? What if intention and grace were different manifestations of Being in the form of INDIVIDUAL SUPPORT AND COSMIC SUPPORT?

Maybe we are the organs of Being, we are its eyes, its ears, its heart, its hands.

Perhaps our intention and practice and discipline are the ways in which Being manifests itself and creates and knows itself.

Perhaps our practice is the way through which Being manifests truth, beauty and goodness. HERE/NOW.

3.

"Perfect practice" as a technique does not exist.

You are the perfect practice. Your life (your attributive, non-possessive…) is the perfect practice. This perfection is constantly perfected and can be verified through the loosening up and final disappearance of effort and resistance.

The idea that a moment can come when effort and resistance

disappear completely is correct, however, this does not mean that they cannot reappear the next moment.

Hope is a trap

What stops you from being, from being present, is nothing but your hope for the future. Hoping for something to be different keeps you looking for some future fantasy. But it is a mirage; you'll never get there. The mirage stops you from seeing the obvious, the preciousness of Being. It is a great distortion, a great misunderstanding of what will fulfill you.
A.H. Almaas, mystic and author

1.

In the third canto of Inferno in *The Divine Comedy* by Dante Alighieri, the author entering the gates of hell finds these words written, "Leave all hope you who enter."

We can interpret these words as a warning that frightens and depresses us, or we can understand that Dante's journey, as well as ours, is a journey INSIDE, a journey to reunite with Spirit, which begins with the acknowledging of our darkness, of the hidden and un-confessable shadows. And in this journey Dante has Virgil next to him who, in my opinion, is a representation of the inner guide: the ability to know the real without filters and concepts, the capacity for directly experiencing what is exactly as it is.

Hope is recognized, by those who have investigated the mechanism of the egoic mind, as the pole of a fundamental duality that defines all mental activity: rejection and hope. Rejection of what is and hope for something different, and how this continuous and compulsive internal movement would recreate separation from the experience of the here/now.

Self-remembering, which is to remember oneself ("emptiness of objects" and "emptiness of the self") and the practice of presence, therefore has two fundamental components that support it:

1. Stop rejecting.
2. Stop hoping... and perhaps Dante knew.

So, leave all hope you who enter, and the Real is here/now.

2.

HOPE, even in a thousand disguises, is almost for everyone at the center of the Great Search. Hope for enlightenment, for cessation of suffering, for eternal peace, for perfect relationships, for transcendence of survival – everyone has his own and of course each hope reveals the existence, often unconscious or hidden, of the other pole the REJECTION. Rejection of what we live, of what we feel, of what we think, of what we act, of our body, of emotions, of our tendencies and passions, of our desires and drives, in short, REJECTION OF OUR HUMANITY.

And that's why the Great Search is so agonizing for a long time, and why so often we wish we had never started it: we inevitably come to terms with rejection and resistance, the shadow. The carrot of acceptance is then rocked in front of the faces of the young seekers, temporary and apparent resolution of rejection, and it works at least a little, smoothing out the coarsest resistances that concern objects, events, situations. But then at some point, when there's finally the 180-degree turn and the focus starts to turn continuously inside, towards the subject, then it starts to become clear that AS LONG AS I HOPE I ALSO CONTINUE TO INEVITABLY RECREATE REJECTION, the other polarity.

And then we let go of acceptance too and just start RECOGNIZING what is as it is, and the mechanism that continually takes us away from what is takes us to the dead past and to a nonexistent future.

A few nights ago, I watched a TV movie where in confession the priest said to Daredevil: "Being fearless means being hopeless," as if it were a terrible and sinful thing.

IT IS TRUE, BEING HOPELESS IS BEING FEARLESS.

Inertia

Wisdom is subjective knowledge; not so much to know the object as to know the one who knows – this is wisdom. Buddhahood is the transcendence of both. In Buddhahood there are neither object nor subject; duality disappears. There is no one who knows and there is no known; there is no observer or anything to observe – there is only ONE. You can call it whatever you want: you can call it God, you can call it Nirvana, you can call it Samadhi, Satori, whatever you want, only ONE remains. Two dissolves into the One.
Osho, mystic

A seldom acknowledged and even less discussed issue among seekers concerns a fundamental shift that occurs in the mind as an effect of spiritual awakening in relation to its operating efficiency.

In the periods immediately following episodes of awakening, especially the central ones, the mind still tends to resist, mainly passively through a kind of inertia of habits. Osho talked about it, in a discourse he gave, as the need to cultivate enlightenment and to convince the mind that functioning from awakened consciousness is much more efficient than functioning from the conventional mind in everyday life at all levels.

This is an important point because one of the most widespread fears and resistances amongst spiritual seekers concerns precisely the belief that being awakened means somehow losing the ability to navigate the world of form and survival. Basic fears: how will I make the money I need to live? What will happen to my sexuality? Where will my relationships go? If I'm in a state of non-mind, how will I deal with everyday problems? Who will cook, wash the dishes, make the bed again, do the shopping? Will I still be going to the movies? To the gym? Will I drive the car? If I'm completely in the moment, what happens to my plans and projects? And so on.

These questions and the anxiety they contain are understandable and impossible to quiet or satisfy because they are questions that inevitably arise from the reality in which we normally live which is that defined by the past, concepts, beliefs, separation and false identity. Only the direct experience of waking up can give us that completely new and different perspective on ourselves and on reality which clearly shows the absurdity of these fears, the anxiety and the questions themselves.

Fortunately, you do not have to wait for the awakening event – which, by the way, is not only an event but also a process – to recognize that there is a fundamentally fluid and effortless way of living. What we call Direct Experience in the Awareness Intensive and Satori retreats is a dive, mostly temporary, into the Awakened Consciousness in all respects, and allows the participants in the retreats to have a more or less profound, articulated, intense, hilarious taste of what it means to live without identification with personality and ego.

In most cases the inertia of habits and attachment to the known bring us back into identification, and we forget ourselves by often resuming to function mechanically. However, once we have tasted the reality of Being, forgetfulness is more transparent, less dense, less compulsive, I would say almost ramshackle: it is not as mechanical and immediate as it was in the past to fully identify with our problems, our limits, our stories. Something reminds us that we are the subject that experiences the events and objects with which we tend to identify.

If we continue to keep the Koan who is in? or who am I? alive the glue of attachment fails to harden as in the past, and the memory of the moments of absolute presence and freedom lived in the Direct Experience continues to have its scent. Inertia is not absolute.

Five minutes (7)

3:36 p.m.

Who is in?

I write these words and I feel myself landing inside with a sigh of relief which also contains a kind of curiosity... Who is in right now? I smile and feel space that widens around the heart and an I DO NOT KNOW that melts within my organism like honey, sweet and kind, friendly, intimate, playful, innocent, THAT'S IT! Innocent! I close my eyes for a few seconds with joy and voluptuousness... the joy of the darkness inside, of this darkness so serenely welcoming... I don't know... I don't know... I don't know... The back and neck stretch from side to side, and the wind swells the curtain...

3:41 p.m.

Inquiry (7)

1. Explore your concepts, beliefs, opinions and general associations with becoming an adult. What images are you carrying? What are your fears or hopes? Is there resistance to the idea of becoming an adult? Do you think you are already one? Do a fully open investigation without looking for endpoints, open this box and see what's in it.

2. What relationship do you see between what you're finding and your family history?

3. Explore the question of emotional maturity. Will you allow yourself to feel your emotions? Do you idealize them, repress, express, control, dive into them or hide them? Whatever your particular way of experiencing emotions, do you see ways you can enter into a more intimate and

harmonious relationship with them?

4. Clean up the past. What comes to you when you contemplate this sentence? What relationship do you have with the past, and how do you relate to what you see clearly outdated, compulsively repeated?

5. Showing up is obviously referring to our authenticity, explore.

6. How do you recognize intention in your relationship with the truth? What are the symptoms that make you recognize it, especially in the body? And grace, what experiences do you have?

7. Explore the question of hope and your associations, beliefs, opinions. What effect does it have on you when considering life as hopeless?

8. The inertia of structure and habits: what obvious effects do they produce in your life? What are your most familiar physical symptoms indicative of this inertia? What are your most familiar questions in relation to the fear of awakening?

9. Explore the theme of belonging, how it has shown itself and shows in your life, and how important it is.

Eight

The Miracle of Us

The consciousness in you and the consciousness in me, apparently two, really one, seek unity and that is love.
Nisargadatta Maharaj, mystic

1.

I don't know about you, but as far as I'm concerned, I had a few problems with "humans" for several years. I do not want to generalize but I can certainly say that the relationship rarely had the feeling of "we", and much more that of "me and them". In this "me and them" was an intrinsic sense of separation which was sometimes simple to live with, sometimes a whirlwind of confusion, a deep sense of isolation and alienation. Belonging is something so fundamentally animal and unconscious that, at least in me, it has been for years and years a minefield territory especially because, like many others, the only reality I had learned to recognize as the seat of my belonging was my family. I am not here to tell the thousand and a thousand occasions, beautiful and ugly, that justified my belonging to my family, I am sure that you who are reading have also had countless experiences. My family, not only the narrow one but also enlarging it a little, was easy to love even in the dark moments: welcoming, affectionate, full of support and appreciation and with a relatively light price to pay in exchange for this belonging. Later, when I was over thirty years old, I can also say with absolute certainty that my father saw me, really saw me, saw my soul and recognized my individuality and now, later on, my mother also sees me.

At the same time, from an early age I also felt that the territory of belonging was narrow and limited, and I also felt that I had a long way to go to find where and what I belonged to completely and freely; not for blood ties, for the need of survival or protection, but for spiritual affinity, and above all for life choices in the present.

I am not denying that there are deep bonds determined by blood and belonging to a family, clan, or land. I am saying that there is also something else that manifests itself strongly the more a person becomes an individual, with its uniqueness and integration, which includes much, much more than the past. Belonging is a choice in freedom, not a destiny or an accident.

2.

We, you and I, me, my mother and father and brother and the family I was born in, me and my partner, me and my friends, me and those I work with, me and the people I meet, me and those I don't meet and I'm around, me and the humans who live on this planet, me and the animals and the plants and rocks... us and all of us... this is certainly acutely in focus in my present with all the contradictions, lacerations, misunderstandings, fears, expectations, desires, possibilities, miracles, love and fragility, and absolute inextricable interdependence.

Let's get out of the cave – 1

There are more things in heaven and earth, Horatio, than are dreamt in your philosophy.
William Shakespeare, author

Or that we can imagine, and our fear try to prevent. Or our laws manage to control.

Let's get out of the cave of fear and isolation. Let's get out of the cave of the past and habit. Let's come out of the cave of distance, of betrayal, of hiding ourselves, from ourselves first; the cave made of all those things that we repeat to make ourselves small, or to feel superior. The cave of things not said to those we love, or things said with anger, resentment, manipulation. The cave of abandoned dreams, repressed flames, cowardice passed off as wisdom. The cave of the postponement to tomorrow when everything will be fine. The cave where we delude ourselves that we have things under control.

The world as we have known it is falling apart and every personal cave is inevitably shaking. Our ideas, expectations, beliefs, whatever they may be, are tested by a planet that refuses to destroy itself, by a life that has no boundaries, righteous ways, morals. A life that manifests itself in infinite, unpredictable and original forms, and possibilities.

Now is not the time to hide and close. Now is the time to recognize that, within any constraint and limitation, each of us is also completely and absolutely free; free to choose to admit to himself what he really feels. Free to tell others, even if inside him that familiar voice resounds and repeats to him that, "You do not say these things," that he should keep them close to himself and secret.

Free to find delicate and profound ways to communicate with new, spontaneous, loving gestures our existence and the miracle of this breath, of the song of a bird outside the window, of the fear of not being there tomorrow, or of the fear that you will not be there tomorrow.

Now it's time to open ourselves up, to hear what's going on in our hearts, in our bellies, in our genitals, in our skin, in our muscles, in our desires. To listen with the same attention and respect that we give ourselves to what happens to others, when they are in front of the unknown that is existence. Right now.

This existence that exists now as and through me, you, us, all of us, all that is.

Everything, absolutely everything. The air we breathe, the water with which we wash our hands, we who wash them, the virus that seeks carriers, the sun that is starting to warm this part of the planet or that is setting.

Let's get out of the cave – 2

Consistency, predictability, constancy, etc. are social values that have their value and need as we navigate daily life and its social contracts and, at the same time, have zero value when mandatory, if we are obedient and respectful robots that unknowingly bend to the so-called collective need, while deluding themselves of the capacity to have "freedom of choice".

If the freedom conditioned by restrictions in which we live as embodied forms of Spirit is not guided and supported by the absolute freedom of Being, by the awareness of our presence here/now and the direct experience of I AM, then that conditioned and idealized freedom of choice is just a story that we tell ourselves and that we pitifully share with others. A lollipop, a pacifier to gratify ourselves and stay asleep.

Energetically our field is unlimited, connected, receptive, interdependent, communicates incessantly, knows, evolves, and creates.

Language traps

Whenever I think about thinking, my thoughts become words. It is language talking to me. But the language came from outside. I think I control it, but it controls me back... language becomes part of the background noise, the air I breathe, gravity; it's just there... Language shapes us without our understanding how we are being shaped.
Orson Scott Card, author

These days I frequently stumble into a statement, mostly made by "spiritual seekers" of various kinds: "I have learned/I am learning to do nothing." In some it is also accompanied by underlines such as "doing nothing is the most difficult thing", or how they succeeded in doing nothing "with great effort", perhaps also adding a quote from a master or a wise man, Osho, Buddha or Zarathustra.

I wonder if any of them asked themselves, what am I saying? Is it possible that I'm just repeating something I've heard? Is IT REALLY POSSIBLE TO LEARN TO DO NOTHING?

The language we use unconsciously shows our understanding, or not, of our experience and, upon arriving at some point, it is necessary that we learn to listen to ourselves and recognize things that we say mechanically that do not really reflect our personal experience. And maybe even to ask ourselves if we really understood what the teachers said or if we filtered it, as is often the case, through our conditioning.

DOING NOTHING indicates one simple thing: the cessation of doing and implies an absence. How can we learn to do nothing? Doesn't learning mean there's something to learn? That there is an object/event/practice that is learned? How can I learn an absence? It's like saying that I CREATE THE DARKNESS. But isn't darkness also an absence, to be exact the absence of light? When I want darkness, I turn off the light, I act on something that is existentially a presence.

In the same way we cannot learn to do nothing, we can simply learn to stop doing, and then of course there is nothing to do. Then it is possible that it will take a lot of effort to stop doing because a central element of our ego structure is identification with the idea that I AM THE DOER, and this identification is difficult and tiring to let go of, especially as it is supported by everything around us.

The coronavirus has attacked the foundation of this idea of ours, and all the habits and beliefs that support it. Will we be able to take this challenge and go beyond doing? ... Perhaps to Being?

Masters, Mastery and Self-inquiry

Your expectation of something unique and dramatic, of some wonderful explosion, is merely hindering and delaying your Self Realization. You are not to expect an explosion, for the explosion has already happened – at the moment when you were born, when you realized yourself as Being-Knowing-Feeling.
Nisargadatta Maharaj, mystic

1.

Around the end of the previous century, I woke up. What I mean is that I stopped searching and started finding. And what you will be reading is my personal experience as I continued to know myself by being myself. I'll be brief.

I have been practicing mastery for many years; this has been, and still is my absolute passion and endeavor. After waking up a couple of things became obvious. The first was that the journey had just begun and, as someone said, "After awakening, the laundry." Another was the question, "How do I day after day embody self-remembering? How do I learn to accept getting lost and then practice coming back home over and over until the road is so familiar that it starts happening by itself?" One more was, "How do I practice being present and disappearing at the same time, taking myself out of the way?"

This is what Mastery is. What often is called The Second Satori: the conscious and familiar capacity to go back home at will. Getting lost does not cease but it is not a problem as I know the way home. Fear disappears. However, mastery it is still a process.

My way home is self-inquiry. Something I have been practicing for at least forty years; inquiry with the existential Koans, inquiry with the regular Koans of the Zen tradition and inquiry with all kinds of questions and about every aspect of my life, experience, understanding. I love inquiry and I am forever grateful that many Masters have shared this formidable tool.

Inquiry is so much who I am now that I do not really need to practice it other than for fun. Inquiry happens by itself and then something arises as revelation. I do not know where it comes from. What I know is that it brings peace, trust, realization, integration.

A Master is a miracle. A miracle of stability and easiness. There is no self-reflection. Satori has become Samadhi (complete integration), therefore there is no coming and going. A Master is not present, rather he/she is pure Presence. Mastery is possibly and sometimes probably the way to become a Master, God willing.

I know all this as, in mastery, I am completely unified in Being and therefore with all the Masters, and especially Osho, my love.

I am also very attached to mastery because, even though at times I may still create Karma, I can also continue to experience the delight of being a disciple and avoid complete aloneness.

2.

After I woke up many people asked me to give Satsangs. I refused. I looked honestly and intimately within myself, and I saw without any doubt or devaluation that that was not my path. I was not a Master; I was just on the way to Mastery.

I am sure that that decision was one of the smarter ones I have made in my life, and I am also well aware it was not me who made that decision but rather it was Life itself.

Guidance has been with me as long as I can remember, in all the turns I have taken that have shaped my becoming as well as, more fundamentally, my capacity to remember myself.

I am not a Master, but I can certainly function through Mastery.

This functioning has some experiential understandings at its core that shape my embodiment of the Truth.

a.   Whatever existence throws at me has one and only one function, to take me home and show me repeatedly that I am loved.

b.   Everything in life is an opportunity and a challenge to experience, comprehend and manifest the uniqueness that I AM.

c.   I am here bringing a specific gift, embodying and sharing the fundamental Unity of All.

d.   My way is surrendering to innocence. The way to surrendering is submission to what is.

e.   I can make all the mistakes I want because mistakes do not exist.

f.   Freedom is both at the same time: absolute (I AM) and relative (within constraints, in the form).

g.   I know what it means to be present yet only sometimes I am Presence.

h.   To have a drink (see Trungpa Rinpoche and Gurdjieff) and watch a basketball game (see LeBron and the Lakers) is okay... I am HUMAN.

i.   I am not waiting for the next life to be myself.

j.   I do understand what Osho points to when he says, "I am an ordinary man."

k.   Life is good. RIGHT NOW!

3.

Awakening does not mean stopping cleaning. On the contrary, Awakening is just a blip in a process that most of us are already very proficient with.

Mastery is a deep and steadfast dedication to deal with what Osho calls, "The inertia of habits." Mastery is most of all in fact the willingness and capacity to shine the light of awakened consciousness in all the corners of oneself and to include all the shadows and the rejected parts of ourselves as they transform in the love of this surrender to all that we are.

It is a deep surgery where we UNLEARN THE MIND.

In a discourse somebody asked Osho what the relationship between unlearning and meditation was. The answer was (and I quote), "There is no relationship. Unlearning IS meditation. What do we do in fact when we meditate? We unlearn the mind."

The fundamental difference is that as we do not seek anything special anymore, all that energy which is usually occupied in chasing something in particular becomes available to be with what is and notice what needs to be cleaned up. And most of the time we are happy cleaners as we like it light and fun, right?

One of the basic tools in Mastery is a sense of humor as we learn not to take ourselves seriously. We let go of dramas, comparison, self-judgment, goals.

Mastery is consciously UNLEARNING THE MIND DAILY, letting go of all sorts of self-deception, self-justification, self-pity, and self-importance.

Our broom is self-inquiry which is the willingness to tell myself the truth about myself.

Self-inquiry is a radical invitation to the Mystery to reveal itself, and remember, remember, remember.

4.

As we use the inquiry broom, old ideas about ourselves start falling. Identification with the past tends to be released and our self-image becomes more and more transparent. Be aware, SELF-IMAGE DOES NOT DISSOLVE IN MASTERY, IT IS STILL THERE BUT WE CAN SEE THROUGH IT. We can see through our defenses, through our reactivity and projections. We become clearer, more candid, more direct, more open. And we become also ready day after day to face a fundamental obstacle: our desire of BEING SPECIAL. Wanting to be seen, recognized, appreciated, loved as special.

You might perhaps not be telling it even to yourself that this is what you want: being special, and if that is the case it is understandable; for many, most people, this is one of the deepest taboos. And yet, when we look inside with compassion and honesty it is not difficult to recognize this need. Everything grows better with care and attention, and we do intuitively know that. Unfortunately, specialism becomes a wound masked in many ways and, much more fundamental, it is a daily forgetfulness of our True Nature. As in our nature we are all incomparably UNIQUE.

There is a very simple truth that we need to take in our hearts: AS LONG AS WE WANT TO BE SPECIAL, WE WILL NEVER BE FREE AND CONTENT.

Mastery means to consciously move away from specialism and start RECOGNIZING, EMBODYING AND SHARING THE UNIQUENESS THAT EACH ONE IS.

Uniqueness does not know comparison.

Uniqueness does not idealize hierarchies.

Uniqueness does not hold back for tomorrow.

Uniqueness is not afraid as there are no errors possible, just steps into more and more uniqueness.

Uniqueness is diving daily in the mystery of I AM.

5.

How do we know when we are practicing Mastery?

There are a few signs that I recognize in myself and in others.

No need to explain myself

No need to justify myself

No need to hide the truth about myself to myself and to the others, most of the time

No need to play victim

Not knowing is a joy and a blessing

Everything becomes fluid and unpredictable ·

I continuously let go of my personal history

It is fun to be myself

It is exhilarating to recognize myself
It is natural to share myself
I feel grateful and innocent

Five minutes (8)

10:17 a.m.

Who is in?

Deep breath and the Koan going down in the belly. The thought goes to the webinar that begins in a few hours. I'm happy and excited. The sun passes through the venetian blind and touches the floor and my left shoulder. Today is a good day! I feel alive, and alert. I feel gratitude flowing inside me and warmth and... short pause to feel more intimately what is inside and who feels it. It's me! It's me! It's me who hears, and I write, and I think, and I contemplate, and... everything, everything, everything! I look at the clock and realize that I have time and that I am writing fast... time, time, even that's me, it's me who creates it and I live it... another deep breath as I let go all that... short interruption... mind stopped... eyes close in peace and then reopen... I feel the wind and my butt well planted on the chair... The gravity that sustains me... and gratitude possessing and filling me... Who is in? Thank you, Koan, thank you, thank you.

10:22 a.m.

Inquiry (8)

1. How do you recognize when you're closing yourself to the world, to other people, to what's going on? What are the physical symptoms and emotions, the thought-forms, the internal atmosphere? What are the most obvious effects on your life?

2. Explore your experience and understanding of being open to yourself. How do you recognize your inner availability

and what effect it has in your daily life?

3.	Explore your beliefs and concepts with respect to consistency and reliability. Also explore where certain ideas come from, and whether they coincide with your experience of yourself or not. Explore how these beliefs manifest themselves in the image you present to the world. You need absolute candor in doing this inquiry, and the will to tell yourself the truth without compromise is fundamental.

4.	What's your relationship to doing nothing?

5.	Explore your associations to the word Master. Any projections, positive and negative. Expectations, prejudices, yearning. See where you go when you open this box, what's going on within you.

6.	Self-inquiry? What is your understanding of this technique? What relationship do you have with it? What practice or lack of practice? Are there any specific blocks you can detect? Are you available for practice alone but not with others?

7.	Explore how resistance allowed you to make choices that might have gone against your conditioning, the power of others, the education you received, etc. Note what happens if you look at the resistance with appreciation, even if there is rejection, denial, avoidance to do so, and include them in your appreciation.

Nine

Resistance

The revolution wants only one war, the one inside the spirits that abandon to the past the old, bloody roads of the earth.
P.P. Pasolini, film director and poet

One of the biggest obstacles we find in our spiritual journey is our attachment and investment in resistance. We often painfully learn that resistance to "what is" is what makes life stressful, conflicted, full of friction and lack of clarity. So, let's learn to let go of our resistance and to accept, or rather, realize the "suchness" of every moment.

And yet, wasn't it resistance that led us to the search in the first place? Resistance to conditioning, obedience, mediocrity, and so on? Was it not resistance that generated the first doubt about what we were told to join, who we are and how we should be? Is not the desire for truth and authenticity infused with resistance to false authority and the various attempts to brainwash us? To bend and possess our spirit? Is real change possible, not only inside but also outside, without resistance? Is resistance not a fundamental tool to transform our inner relationship with our superego and with the attempts of society to control more and more aspects of our lives?

And is resistance not closely linked to our ability to consciously say NO? And to use our strength to protect and promote life rather than destroy it?

We need to look deep inside and ask ourselves how we can create a new world if we ideologically reject resistance – if we are not willing to take risks by going down that narrow and dangerous road where our spiritual understanding is forged in the fire of life and its uncertainty. How can we bring more awareness, skill, and embodiment to our resistance, while we recognize everything as always-already perfect?

How much do you want to be free?

You don't have to be a man to fight for freedom. All you have to do is to be an intelligent human being.
Malcolm X, revolutionary

This is an uncomfortable and inevitable question.

Freedom is not an ideal, it is not a future goal, it is not something that anyone can give you or will give you; it is an embodied understanding and a practice of personal responsibility about YOUR life, now and every moment.

When we make freedom something to conquer one day in the future; when we continue to expect freedom to be given to us by someone or something, whether it is a new social contract or a magical spiritual event called enlightenment; when we find excuses or reasons to escape this question, it just means that we don't really want to acknowledge that we're not free. And that freedom is not very high on our daily shopping list.

WE'RE free OR WE'RE NOT.

There is no grey area in freedom because freedom is always and already our True Nature. The confusion is in the personality and concepts, ideas, beliefs, idealizations that we carry with us and with which we struggle.

When you understand through a direct experience that YOU ARE FREEDOM and that you can't be anything else, then you are free even within the constraints of daily life.

That is when the question of absolute responsibility combines with absolute freedom. Every moment you are free in your anger, fear, beauty, intelligence, jealousy and gratitude... there is nothing else but freedom. And YOU are the embodied manifestation of it.

The only way to get to know yourself is TO BE YOURSELF IN FREEDOM.

What about the freedom to do nothing?

To do only what has been done before is to live in the shadow of other men.
Anonymous

In recent years there has been a debate that is often very heated and full of obscure predictions about what will happen when production is almost completely operated by Artificial Intelligence. What will happen to all the people who are no longer going to work? How will they feel? How will they fill their days? What will the meaning of life be without work? And what happens to those Constitutions that, like the Italian one, are based on work? Of course, all these more or less gloomy scenarios are theoretical and based on humanity as we know it; the one defined by the Industrial Revolution and, much less, by the IT revolution. Yes, free time... everyone complains that they don't have enough... and now? Now that the virus has thrown us into the REALITY of being responsible for our time, now what? Fundamental questions arise, such as those from Chapter 2:

Who am I if I don't *do*? If I do not produce, if I do not manifest myself through the achievement of goals, the planning of programs for the future, competition with others?

What is the point of my life when time and space are determined not by external factors but by my presence? By my ability to be here/now?

Who am I if the social labels I typically define myself with don't work? If I can't go around showing off the new car, the signed purse, my jewelry, or cheering for my favorite team.

The virus is destroying our self-definitions, the social images that we have cultivated for decades, the small and large certainties that we surround ourselves with so as not to feel the precariousness and novelty of every moment.

The virus is anticipating a world where we are not in control and where the human myth of bending nature to its wills fails miserably.

The virus is showing us that having time for oneself is not easy if we don't take responsibility for being ourselves.

FREE TIME brings together two fundamental words, Time and Freedom.

If we do not recognize that time is created by us, that time is a manifestation of our awareness and presence, that time, as Einstein has told us for decades, is relative to the subject of experience – without this awareness, the second word Freedom is meaningless and above all impossible to embody.

The virus is challenging something much deeper than our body and our health; it is challenging our EXISTENCE, our ability to exist and not just to survive.

Self-pity

Self-pity is easily the most destructive of the non-pharmaceutical narcotics; it is addictive, gives momentary pleasure and separates the victim from reality.
John Gardner, author

Self-pity is one of the most powerful and insidious obstacles that a spiritual seeker will encounter sooner or later if one observes honestly.

Self-pity is often hidden from those who practice it and manifests itself indirectly through complaining about others making them responsible for our pains and sufferings, or as an attitude of inflexibility and a sense of being on the side of reason, and also with a great capacity for self-deception. As long as there is a crumb of self-pity, there is no total assumption of responsibility for our life and experience.

When the responsibility is not total, freedom also cannot be total.

This attitude (open or hidden) of self-pity creates a lack of strength, purpose and will, that waters down the search and sabotages the flame of our passion. For centuries we have been accustomed to waiting for the miracle, to be saved. We are accustomed to being enslaved by our superego. For too long we have been accustomed to the decadence of form and the lack of attention to content, for too many years we have refined the art of not taking responsibility and we have thus lost the true basis of our dignity.

Until we get rid of self-pity, we will be slaves to each other, to our minds and to our history. "When I close my eyes, I am completely motionless and I do not overlay concepts with the pure presence of what is, there is no self-reflection, there is no time and space, there is no inside and out, there is no ego or enlightenment but the simple and direct realization of what is." To this statement of mine one of my friends and students replied: "It depends on who closes their eyes..." and this is the most classic mistake of seekers: to think that True Nature is only available to some, only in some moments, only if certain situations are present, etc. This is not the case: our True Nature is not only INEVITABLY ALWAYS PRESENT but moreover manifests itself in our everyday life countless times in countless ways. It is merely that we do not notice it or, if we notice it, we immediately shift attention to the habit of limitation and personality, in short to what is familiar. Very often in fact we experience the eternal here/now which is not infinite time but absence of the concept of absolute time in the here/now. Very often we are beyond the subject/object separation and in a state of merging, with a book, with what we cook, with music, with our body, with a mouthful of water, with a cat or a loved one... only that it is so "ordinary" that it is not part of our idealization of non-separation. Very often there is no self-reflection but there is direct experience of ourselves and the object which at that moment appears in awareness: a sensation, a feeling, the steering wheel of the car, the hand of your man or your woman or a child, but this doesn't fit with the idealization of spiritual realization.

Idealization of spiritual realization: this is the trickiest nightmare.

TRUE REALIZATION INCLUDES EVERYTHING, CONTINUOUSLY, WITHOUT DISTINCTION. Realizing the shadow of compulsive behavior has the same value as realizing a divine aspect because in GOD, in THE ABSOLUTE, in PRIMARY AWARENESS, there is no distinction of value between shadow and light, personality and authentic Self.

STOP DIVIDING, dear friend, and creating pseudo-spiritual hierarchies.

EVERYTHING IS DIVINE, YES, NOW AND ALWAYS.

Celebrating death

Death is the only wise advisor that we have. Whenever you feel, as you always do, that everything is going wrong and you're about to be annihilated, turn to your death and ask if that is so. Your death will tell you that you're wrong; that nothing really matters outside its touch. Your death will tell you, "I haven't touched you yet."
Don Juan Matus, mystic and Yaqui sorcerer

I was at home that night when shortly after seven o'clock someone, I don't remember who, came to tell me that Osho had left the body and that I had to run to Buddha Hall.

I was one of his photographers and one of his guards. My job was to stand next to the podium where they would display his body and then accompany him to the Ghats on the river where the funeral pyre would be prepared.

I was there, standing, completely incredulous, shocked, overwhelmed with pain and even somewhat strangely surprised, when they brought the body into Buddha Hall and rested it where his chair usually was for discourse.

I expected, hoped, I wished with all my heart that it was just another one of his jokes and that, suddenly, he would rise as had happened in some of the stories of Zen masters that he had told us for years.

Here I am! I'm still here! He would have said...

But it didn't happen, Osho wouldn't get up, he wouldn't smile, his body wasn't breathing and everything in me became icier, moment by moment.

I was there when we lifted the coffin and took it out of the ashram amid tears and chants, dancing and sobs, candles, guitars and drums, celebrating our beloved, our master, and our fear and loss.

I was there when the flames started lapping his body, and I was there when they went out leaving only ashes.

I was there also when, a few years earlier, he said he was going to leave when we were ready. And I was there when every night, at the end of his discourse, he would be guiding us with absolute intensity and love beyond form, asking us to die and be alive again.

For ourselves and for this mysterious universe.

Freedom, oh freedom!

The mind creates the abyss, the heart crosses it.
Nisargadatta Maharaj, mystic

In everyday life this question of freedom can be confusing and painful. If we try to "solve" it through the mind and its limited capacity for understanding we are destined to fail – as Suzuki Roshi says, "the monkey-mind that tries to describe enlightenment!"

From that perspective, there is only duality: either I am free, or I am not, and/or a confused gradation of freedom based on dualistic concepts. In the context of the mind, the question of freedom, like many others, remains an irresolvable and irreconcilable dilemma. Surrendering to what is means then not to fall into the trap of dualism and let go of any effort aimed at finding solutions. We open ourselves to include paradox in everyday life. Essentially this means recognizing the complementary and existential synchronicity of two aspects of freedom:

We are absolutely free in Being that "is all it is". This absolute freedom is impersonal, complete, eternal, indefinable and incommunicable. This dimension of the Real is represented by the vertical line of the here/now, the eternal that is beyond time.

We are free "within restrictions" in the form, in the manifestation that we embody in daily life when, unaware of our hypnosis of separation, we believe we exist as a separate self that makes choices. This dimension of the Real is represented by the horizontal time/space line.

In fact, we find ourselves every moment, conscious or not, in the center where vertical and horizontal intersect, the living expression of a continuous resurrection, of the endless creation that manifests itself every moment.

What does it mean to us from the point of view of "practice"?

Keeping the Koan present in our conscious mind as consistently as possible, we remain in contact with the paradox: when we remember, who is in? we rest in the realization that there is no separate entity and there is no inside and outside (vertical line). At the same time, we realize that this impersonal presence is embodied in each of us: it is I who live this life (horizontal line).

This pure presence that I can express as I AM, as embodied, is colored with qualities, nuances, aspects, possibilities, in the flow of time/space, and I recognize the concrete possibility of consciously participating in evolution, mine, yours, ours, of the universe in which I live.

The paradox cannot be "solved", nor does it need to be solved. It can only be experienced, and regarding "how" to live it there are dozens of approaches, expressions of different mystical schools, which are more or less effective, more or less articulated and more or less elegant.

Attachment to Direct Experience

One thing: you have to walk and create the way by your walking; you will not find a ready-made path. It is not so cheap, to reach to the ultimate realization of truth. You will have to create the path by walking yourself; the path is not ready-made, lying there and waiting for you. It is just like the sky: the birds fly, but they don't leave any footprints. You cannot follow them; there are no footprints left behind.
Osho, mystic

My first Awareness Intensive Retreat as a participant took place around thirty years ago, and since then I have participated in many Retreats and Intensives. As a facilitator I have also accompanied many people on their journey. What is even more fundamental to me, is that existential Koans live in me, embodied, in my blood, in my bones, in my muscles, in my functioning: I breathe, Who is in? Who is in? moves me. I meditate, Who am I? My scent is Who am I?

At some point in my journey, I wrote this poem referring to direct experience:

It comes and strikes you.
Your eyes suddenly open to see that which is,
the world is transfigured and everything

is resplendent with the grace of God.
Or it comes as a gentle whisper,
soft as a breeze that flows under your skin
and melts your bones.
Different cords vibrate inside you
and the music of existence
plays without a player.
It takes possession of your body, changing
the direction of the streams of energy,
rounding corners, rewiring nerves,
helping the hidden smile appear
on your lips and innocence to moisten your eyes.
The secret heart fills with sweet, gentle longing as you
see the true face of the Beloved
in the thousands of small things of everyday life.
You don't want anything special
when everything is just perfect.
Preciousness becomes the name of the
game. Every form is the form of
the Beloved.
Every name is His name.
Nothing can be excluded, ever.
Neither when you remember, nor when you
forget.

This is the magic of the direct experience, its unpredictable nature and manifestation, always new, always different; and how it is every moment we are present.

One of the most beautiful and indescribable gifts of facilitating the retreats is to witness the blossoming of Being like a phoenix from the ashes when I sit in one-to-one interviews with participants. The Truth comes alive in all its freshness, uniqueness and glory, and is embodied in the person I sit before.

How could we not get attached to such splendor? And in fact,

I remember my second intensive and the expectations, the flame of the yearning that burned inside, the desire at all costs to taste again, again, that experience! What a curse! To know deeply that the past is dead, that there is no possibility that it will happen again, that I cannot in any way produce, manipulate, control the possibility of direct experience happening again, yet try and strive in every way.

As I heard Osho say, it's like when we pull a fish out of the ocean and throw it on the beach – the pain and suffering and despair it feels, the trying at all costs and the effort to get back into the ocean to which it belongs; it is part of the ocean and can't stay away from it.

What I saw and felt within, I also saw and heard in other seekers as they found themselves sitting with the Koan again and again, and glimpsed the real possibility of immersing themselves in that incredible dance of Intention and Grace.

Once we have tasted the direct experience of our true nature, once we have experienced the spaciousness and lightness of Being, once we have heard the silence of the mind, once we have felt the fusion with everything that is, even for a few moments, it is impossible to forget and above all it is evident that we can go back Home. We can be who we really are.

I remember reading what Buddha often repeated about the search and the possibility of having firsthand experience of oneself... that it was a tragedy not to start the journey and an even greater tragedy not to end it. In the period between the beginning of the journey and the apparent end the Koan is our stick and our light, and we feel addicted, and in fact we are, until a miraculous absolute identity with the Koan takes place. At that moment, immediately, direct experience is the reality in which we live, the air we breathe, our own life and awareness. Dealing with attachment to the direct experience is necessary and an inevitable step on the way.

What I have also experienced and seen in many others is

that at some point the intelligence of grace begins to dissolve expectations and attachment, and an increasingly stable and joyful condition of submission to the Real happens.

This submission is a continuous and delicate invitation to mystery, and the recognition that the end does not exist while we immerse ourselves more and more in the mystery of Who is in.

… and finally…

The sense of identification

The identification process moves in two directions simultaneously.

The first is the one that is most generally emphasized: the movement through which we lose the connection with our subjectivity and identify with an object of our experience, both external like a person, an event, an object that we possess, as well as internal, a thought, an emotion, a feeling, our history and so on. This is also the dynamic that we most easily tend to recognize because the effects of losing connection with the sense of ourselves can be very powerful.

The other aspect/direction of the identification process is subtler, more hidden and generally less recognized if we do not pay attention directly to it. It has to do with the fact that every object with which we identify becomes in turn a brick of our sense of identity: this is me because I have this thought, this emotion, this memory, this opinion, etc. Literally: I RECOGNIZE MYSELF AND DEFINE MYSELF THROUGH THE OBJECTS WITH WHICH I IDENTIFY. This identification allows me to delude myself into knowing who I am, and this belief is a most fundamental egoic self-deception.

For this reason, even long-time spiritual seekers rarely really engage in contemplating who am I? Or who is in? To ask these questions is inevitably to start considering the real possibility of not knowing, of having absolutely no answer. It means possibly entering a spiral of doubt, uncertainty, fragmentation and identity crises. And this is precisely the case because working permanently with an existential Koan induces a progressive disidentification with the objects of experience, whatever they may be, and at the same time an ever-faster recognition that in the absence of objects even the presumed subject of experience tends to dissolve.

At that point the question of identity becomes impossible to avoid: do I need an identity to exist? Or can I realize my existence regardless of an identity?

The truth that manifests itself is paradoxical: on the one hand the complete disappearance of subject, object and their separation; on the other absolute presence of the One without two. The identity based on separation disappears and the absolute identity based on unity is revealed.

Sensuality

One of the clearest and most obvious symptoms of our becoming present has to do with our senses.

Compulsive identification with mental processes, with past and future, with concepts, ideals, images, expectations and, in general, with control, manifests itself over time through a progressive limitation of our sensitivity. Our senses atrophy, harden, excluding everything that does not confirm our description of reality, inside and out. We only see what is allowed to see, we only hear what coincides with certain frequencies, when we touch and are touched a thousand old barriers prevent energy from flowing freely in giving and receiving. We have almost lost our sense of smell and we cannot "smell" what manifests itself in the moment or, if we do, we attach to it judgment, evaluation, opinions almost immediately. And in the same way it becomes almost impossible to "savor" what existence offers us and move slowly, while we perceive how the force of gravity sustains us and the force of grace raises us. Meditation is a wonderfully powerful tool to re-sensitize ourselves, to get rid of the dry skin of habits and attachment to the old. The most important step is the radical shift of attention from objects to the subject: the one who feels, sees, savors, listens, touches, perceives, and this is where the Koan Who is in? revolutionizes our universe.

This radical transformation takes place through three steps:

The focus shifts, from being focused mainly on the objects of experience and their continuous and incessant change, to the subject of experience. This shift induces the recognition that Awareness embodied in the subject is not part of the movement in time/space but exists in the present/eternal, in the vertical of the here/now.

The second has to do with a radical change in our senses that from being exclusive become inclusive, functioning as neutral receptors of what is there. The filters they typically operate through gradually dissolve, allowing us much more lively and dynamic perceptions.

Finally, the third has to do with our reconnection with the spiritual senses and their alignment with the physical senses. Spiritual senses work naturally, unconditioned: without filters, without past, without evaluation, without boundaries and separation. The Real is no longer a description created over time but a receiving and understanding of what manifests in its objectivity now, in this moment.

The manifesting of these passages, even when temporary, is filled with sensuality. Literally! We perceive ourselves, others, the things around us, the air we breathe, the movement in space, the light, the sounds, as a living and luminous presence in which we are immersed and in which we are participants and co-creators. The world is transfigured and shines divinely. We rediscover the innocent amazement of seeing, feeling, listening, moving, touching; smells and flavors become alive, immediate and fascinating again. And we ask ourselves: how could I forget?

Beyond Direct Experience

The expression Direct Experience is at the same time a blessed and unfortunate expression. When we start practicing with existential Koans, Direct Experience gives us, or rather gives our mind, something to chew on, a possible goal, a direction, something to aspire to, and this helps us to focus on the intention and crystallize our will, embody our passion and yearning. As the Koan gradually burns through our resistance, our expectations, our concepts and beliefs, little by little our structure begins to melt, to become more porous, more welcoming and transparent, less dense. The glue of attachment and identification shows its impotence to recognize the truth of our True Nature and frustration becomes our best friend.

Little by little the tension of the search begins to leave our body, our muscles, our bones while body and energy begin to spontaneously align in the vertical of gravity and grace, and a simple, natural sense of dignity and integration emanates from our presence.

Little by little the voice that speaks is not only yours or mine, but also that of everyone, indeed, that of the whole, and what it says expresses without doubt or reserves what is, here/now.

Little by little the spaciousness of the mystery, its vastness and dynamism fill every cell, every movement, every silence, every look.

"I" disappears. "You" disappears. "We" disappears. All that remains is TATHATA, the suchness of what it is.

The idea that there is an experience separate from the one who is living and perceiving it dissolves.

The Direct Experience disappears undone in the presence of the ONE without two.

And everything falls in tune.

Loving the Koan: Experiences of finders on the path

Sudasi Helen Anderson
General Manager, Capability, Telstra,
Melbourne, Australia

Who is in? Sharing how valuable and nurturing this Koan is for me.

I love the name of this chapter "finders on the path". It really sums up one of the ways I find the Koan valuable – it turns me into an eternal finder, and by definition an eternally curious seeker. "Finder" is optimistic, it implies there is something to find and explore and there is! I remember returning home after one of the Satori retreats where I'd journeyed through the most vibrant, dynamic, dark, light, tumultuous and exhilarating range of experiences, and returning to my home I felt lost and empty. I felt despondent and shared this with Avikal in a conversation soon after, and he said, "Yes, but who is experiencing the lostness?" The mystery, joy and opportunity that question created offered me the reminder that realizing that there is an "experiencer" is the greatest joy of the Koan for me.

It reminds me again and again. Every time I remember to be the Koan, take it inside and explore I realize that I AM, there is a subject noticing. That probably sounds a little esoteric and spiritual. I am a very practical person. And in practical terms what the Koan does is continue to ground me and have me return again and again to the present. "Hmm, so?" you say. Well, the present is the only moment I can actualize and be in. So, when I am not the Koan I have abandoned myself to either a story of the past, or a story of the future.

If it is a story of the past, based on my habitual patterns developed over many years of conditioning I will have a range of *Groundhog Day* experiences; reliving when someone did me harm, wasn't fair, how my family structure impacted me. This results in false evidence appearing to be real (in my mind) and leaves me feeling justified to wallow in victimhood.

If the story is based on the future, I am imagining what may or may not happen, and depending on whether I am feeling optimistic or pessimistic I may be experiencing a lofty exciting future, or a depressing "no way, great things like that aren't available for me". So, in the non-present state, when I am not the Koan I am on a roller coaster, and its rhythm and movement is based on my current mood, and state of mind. As you know the mind is always moving, shifting, changing and jumping around so it is an exhausting master who I feel beholden to.

Sometimes, as that whole adventure occurs, I remember the Koan. I stop. I take the Koan inside, "Who is in?", I look, and then describe to myself what I find. Every time I arrive at a place where the folly of having abandoned myself yet again causes me to laugh out loud, and internally I go… "Ahhh, here I am." It is like taking a magic pill, and it brings me to myself again. It doesn't necessarily always land me in a calm peaceful state, that's not the point. It does always land me realizing "I AM", I exist, and I may be noticing that I am experiencing fury, or agitation, or peace or calm, and as I am experiencing those, and including them in my experience, I remember again that I exist, and all is well regardless of the experience.

I don't want to convey that the Koan is all love and roses either. Many times, in the Satori retreats I've cursed the Koan for the winding journey it has taken me on, and over time and with experience I am a more surrendered seeker. The fear of what I might find has moved more to anticipation and curiosity for the mystery that the work with the Koan unfolds.

I have experienced this mystery many times. For example, I will think I've arrived at a gem which explains or sheds light on a pattern that I'd unconsciously been letting drive me and which has created misery in my life. In the first instance I think that's the discovery, however, I often find it's only the surface pattern, and as I continue to explore the deeper, complex protection system that held it up is revealed, and it is always engaging, confounding and gloriously and beautifully creative. I have been bereft with the sheer wonder and joy of my soul and personality, and how they've colluded to protect me. And once I've become aware of that protection and collusion, I have been in awe of how it can be given space, and included in the glorious complexity of who I am. Then, like the monks who work for days creating a beautiful colorful sand mandala, and sweep it away with a swish, it is gone. It is the same with what I have found; it is gone, and I am in another moment.

So, the Koan reminds me of being in an Escher drawing traversing and wandering moment by moment into unknown territory, through odd structures I don't relate to or know; taking one mysterious step at a time. It is a wild ride, and a curious search which enlivens, opens, and blesses me every moment of every day. I embrace the Koan with the curiosity of a child with no expectation of what I might find, and enjoy the ride safe in the knowledge that I AM.

Prem Sharabo
Los Angeles, United States

In her death my mother gave me a second birth.

Some call it Karma and some say we end up in an episode (consciously or unconsciously) because we are ready to reap the realization out of it, whatever that might be. All the events that have happened in my family story created an indelible perception of who I am. Many of my life events have happened around death, sex, society and spirituality. As a child of nine or ten years old, on a festival day when all of the family performed a special prayer to Lord Ganesh, I told my father, "I am not going to pray unless you tell me who this god is and where he is." He tied me to a pole, beat me and left me there for half a day. As I recall now, I was asking myself, "Who is this god? He won't show up if I don't pray?" While I have gone through the pain of many traumatic events, I always asked questions and that's what saved me from getting sucked into the abyss. In nearly every Who is In? and Satori retreat that I participated the Inquiry took a jab at the melancholy I was born into as well as graced me with many peak moments.

From the day she conceived me with anxiety in her womb until her death, my mother remained the central character in my "family story" which was the story of my world. During her later years when a series of dramatic events coincided with my self-inquiry practice, the long painful indifference towards her gradually turned out to be acceptance and enormous love. A week after cremating her I arrived in Slovenia for the Who is In? retreat. Still grieving and tender I began the inquiry. Instead of grieving, in the name of inquiry, I started philosophizing about death, grief, and my fear of being alone in the world since she was my last family member. All my memories of her arose creating an emotional atmosphere inside and an intellectual interpretation outside. But when I had an interview with Jivan, he gently told me that if I needed to, I could let go of the "talk" and just cry. I felt like he punctured the bubble that I was in. For a day or so in every session after that I did nothing but sob. Wave after wave from the bottom of my belly brought out my grief and I became the sorrow. Little by little my heart softened, and still full of tears, the inquiry continued.

All that one has to do in the (practice of) inquiry is to give oneself to it. If we don't manipulate the inquiry to achieve or understand something the tentacles of inquiry spread open by themselves into infinite consciousness. Even if we end up in a crisis the Koan opens a new dimension. Eventually the Koan brought me to a question that I had never encountered until then in my life, "Who am I without my mother?" My mother was the other and I mainly existed in relationship to this other and the story. A few sessions later the inquiry transmuted into, "Who am I without the story of my mother?" The convoluted story that had occupied all of my life and had driven so many episodes that shaped who I am (and also the way I perceived much of myself) started making no sense. Knowing fully that the person around whom the weight of my world history revolved was gone I couldn't relate as a son to someone who was not in her body. "Son" – it was just a title. The story, which had defined me and given me an image and identity in the eyes of others and established a particular perception of the world and myself, was now at stake. More and more as I inquired, the Koan crystallized into "Who am I now without my story?" and each time the 45 years of story flashed in the back of my mind. The story started fading into the background yet remained a provocation, and my attention started shifting towards an intense curiosity of: "Who am I *really* without my story?" In my mind I felt a disassociation between the story and myself. A distance opened. Every memory around her and the family story that popped up in the field of my awareness started floating like a feather and fell like a lone leaf in the pure autumn air. I realized that I have known myself only through my family story, and now without the story I felt lost. Having never been in this kind of situation before I couldn't understand it. As the emotional entanglement with the story started disappearing, I didn't find anything else to say about myself. The thought that if I let go of her and the story there will be nothing, but emptiness frightened me. I see that how I filled my years with her, how I engaged my time with all the events, and now when that is not possible anymore, what would I do with my life? When both attachment and resistance became absent, whom would I fight with? I couldn't explain myself to myself anymore and ended up in a state that was grief, that had no answer, that was helplessness and bewilderment. This state is totally subjective as if my body contained all of them within. In that inability to describe I returned to the awareness of my physical body, my heart space, and a feeling that something had come to an end – all of these simultaneously. There existed no movement. In other words, despite what was going on a reaction was absent. Any attempt I made to answer did not make any sense to myself.

Kranjska Gora is small town nestled in the Slovenian side of the Alps with its endless range of giant mountains and its peaks touching the sky. When it rained, they turned dense black hiding behind heavy clouds that have a primordial right to freely roam among the valleys. They descend to the lower slopes and meadows. Heavy with rainwater they are stillness in movement. The retreat was held at a venue among these mountains. During the nights I would listen, dripping rain on the rooftop window of my room. There was absolute silence, except for the sound of rolling water from a small river that ran by the side of the venue. "Who am I without my story?" The Koan echoed deep inside. Inside that vacuum I was left with no means of exploring any further. Not that I wanted to or planned for it, I arrived in a state of no-action on my part and the Koan remained one with me. Often a curiosity would wake me up in the night and I would wonder, "Who would I be without this story?" or "Who am I?" Except for the Koan rising and falling on its own, there was no other thought. In some remote corner of the world, alone among mountains, the silence of the darkness entered my room and the peace of the night my inner landscape. The inquiry continued into the next day.

As the unwavering intensity of the inquiry continued and power of the Koan penetrated my narcissistic identification with my family, a sense of weightlessness and freedom began to emerge. The freedom was from all that I had gone through during each of the events in my life. Very vaguely I began to feel that I was a separate entity from the story. Soon it became clear that I existed in spite of my story and its intricacies with my life.

Personalization fell to the side and I realized that my story was one of the million stories that were happening all around me. I had a faint recognition, first as a thought and later as a felt-sense of *"I am"* irrespective of the story. As the relationship with the other was retracted a strong *"I-am-ness"* emerged that was independent of any definitions, free of identifications as a son, as an Indian, as a brother, as a victim, and the rest of the labels. There was a fear that I was now alone in the world as well as a fascination when I recognized my existence not through the eyes of the other but my own. I felt like a newborn baby opening its eyes for the first time to the world. A limited perception of the world from the point of view of my story was eliminated. A freedom at this new home I found which is "being myself" and a trembling at the same time since the world started breaking like a flood into the new space which was, until then, filled with the obsessive thoughts of the story. Each time I received the instruction, "Tell me who is in?", it stoked a physical presence of myself and only a self-remembrance would respond. I sat inside of my body watching how the reactions were absent as thoughts rose and fell in my consciousness. Sometimes I would meet the instruction in midair and turn silent. My eyes remained open, but they were actually looking at the expansive emptiness inside. The words, "Mom, thank you, we have met, and thank you, you are gone," came out of my mouth. I could see through the windows that the clouds were gone, countless tall pine trees revealed the majesty of the mountains which belonged to all time – past, present and future. The bright sunlight entered through the windows casting its dancing shadows.

In her death my mother gave me a second birth. This journey of glimpsing who I am as I am couldn't have been possible without two people: Ganga and Avikal. I have been doing Who Is In? and Satori groups with them for some time. While Koan drove me to the roots of a convoluted, decades-long traumatic story, each time I fell into a trap they would help me get out with love and brilliant guidance.

All the Buddhas before us have already said what is needed for the awakening of man. Religion has evolved to a point there is no outside agency needed anymore. If we want to have an authentic experience of who we are, more than looking at something outside of us we need to inquire into our own "self" and find our own truth.

Sattva Margarit Davtian
Life Coach, Los Angeles, USA

Who is in? – (The Ascent)
November 12, 2019

Dear journal,

It happened. It really happened. I almost can't believe that I was there. That that was me. And if Avikal hadn't witnessed it I'd probably think it was just my imagination, maybe I'm going crazy. He said I was right on the edge and all he had to do was just give me a little push. I'm trying to find the words to describe it but there are no words. How can I describe satori? How can I put words to an experience beyond words? I was just there, simply existing. What more is there to say? Who would ever think that simply existing could feel so wildly orgasmic? Who could ever imagine being so turned on by the air? And to think it was so obvious all this time! How could I have missed it?! How could I have not felt so moved by the rain? How could I have not experienced being high off life? How can I look at a bird or see people hugging ever again without this immense joy erupting through my heart and pouring out of my eyeballs? What am I going do with this feeling? How can I possibly go back to normal life with this information? I have to ask Avikal. How do I go back to normal life while being this awake?

Earlier that evening, Avikal had sat in as an observer during a dyadic session with my partner; it was my turn to be a speaker. Our dyadic sessions were exactly 40-minutes long in which two people sat face-to-face from each other and alternated between speaker and listener while asking each other the Koan, "Who is in?" In Zen, a *Koan* is an existential question, riddle, or puzzle that has no answer, meant to provoke "great doubt" by consciously creating a crisis in the mind (i.e. driving you fucking crazy). By continuously asking, "Who is in?" the dyadic exercise becomes an energetic container in which the speaker can have a direct experience of reality and be witnessed in their Truth by the listener.

"I can feel my heart jumping through my chest," I told my partner when Avikal took a seat next to her. I was relieved that I did not have to make eye contact with him. One of the rules of the dyadic exercise is to maintain eye contact with your partner, who served as a mirror. Even so, I could feel Avikal's green eyes burning a hole through my skull and it made me wish that the ground underneath my meditation cushion would split open and swallow me whole.

"My entire nervous system is collapsing," I kept going, surprised at my unabashed honesty. "I just want to run and hide. I hate being watched. But it's also kind of exciting. Now my voice is starting to shake. I'm also aware that I'm rambling. I do that when I'm nervous."

By the 7th day of the Awareness Intensive Teacher Training, I had become surprisingly accustomed and even amused by the panic that would settle into my body whenever Avikal witnessed me in the labyrinth of my messy and ridiculous experience of Who Is In. The presence of my Italian Zen master was confronting, to say the least. I had never felt so emotionally and spiritually exposed. There was a striking intensity in the way that Avikal could read your energy and illuminate the dirt and debris that had gathered on the darkest corners of your psyche, like a fluorescent blacklight beaming against a surface full of invisible stains, undetectable to the naked eye but brought to light by Pure Consciousness. There was no place to run and hide from the spotlight of Avikal's bare gaze. With the simple question, "Who is in?" Avikal could dissect the delicate fibers of your so-called personality in deliberate and efficient strokes with one hand, while gently guiding and supporting the complete unravelling of your personhood with another. Like a Japanese Master Chef with exquisite knife skills, Avikal had mastered the art of cutting you open and exposing the cracks and holes on the surface of your Being. I had never seen grown men weep in the way they wept in front of Avikal. His teaching style was not for the faint of heart, to say the least.

"I'm not here to be liked, I'm not here to be your friend. I'm here to help you experience *satori*," he told the group one day during our training of "Who is in?". "I'm here to challenge something very fundamental – your ideas about freedom. I'm here to ask, who is in?"

Who is in? – The question that would become both my ball and chain and the greatest source of my liberation. It was my second time grappling with the paradox of reality. The first time around had been earlier that year in Pune, India where I had completed a 3-day Who Is In Awareness Intensive retreat at the infamous Osho International Meditation Resort, the birthplace of the controversial movement led by Indian mystic Rajneesh who propagated the teachings and philosophy of one's sexuality and spirituality. Though I had become frustrated with this *Koan* during my first experience with it, it had penetrated my consciousness deeply enough to call me back for more. I saw the Koan as a puzzle that I was determined to hack, and I felt confident and safe under the tutelage of Avikal Costantino who had been one of Osho's disciples during those early years of the Human Potential Movement.

"The conscious choice to evolve is a great adventure," Avikal would say in his delightful Sicilian accent, his face beaming with vitality and childlike mischief, as if letting you in on a naughty little secret. "The seed must destroy itself for the plant to grow. You have to break down to break through. Through struggle, you create the capacity to see. Out of every struggle, something new evolves."

"Who is feeling nervous? Who is being watched? Who wants to run and hide?" Avikal asked me during that particular dyadic session on the 7th day, which happened to be the last session of the last day of our training. These questions were rhetorical, and I was therefore excused from having to answer them. Or so I thought.

I froze.

"Sattva, look at me."

I looked.

"Who is saying all of this?"

"Me," I whispered softly, timidly.

"Say it again. Louder."

"Me," I raised my voice. "ME, ME, ME, ME, ME!" Now I was acting out, as if to beat him to the punch at exposing my insecurities.

"Hang on, don't get hysterical. Why is it so difficult for you to say that?"

I felt embarrassed. Angry. Amused. Excited. All at the same time. My cheeks were flashing hot red, belly full of fire, sweat beads forming on my forehead, dampness in my armpits. Lump in my throat.

"I... I don't know," I stammered. "It feels... lame." I couldn't imagine the answer to the question, "Who is in?" could be as obvious as, "Me." I couldn't believe that it could be so simple, so uncomplicated to crack the Koan. Me? Really? Who is in, is me? Impossible!

"Lame? It's lame to be yourself?" I searched Avikal's face for some hint that he was just pulling my leg. But his face was stern. Sincere, but stern.

At first, I was stupefied by the sheer audacity of this question which seemed to have been hurled at me at 7,000 RPM without warning; my first instinct was to dodge it, to push it away because I didn't want to see what it would reveal to me – something ugly, yet so precious. Something mysterious, yet so familiar. I felt a sense of both urgency and hesitation to rush towards this "something" – to see it, to greet it, what is it? I sat there, bewildered for what seemed like an eternity as time slowed down, way down. It was one of those moments that were gone in an instant but could have lasted forever. It was one of those moments that you never forget. It was a moment of Truth. It was like facing a familiar piece of music but hearing it for the very first time.

I looked into Avikal's large, dilated pupils which had become a prism-like reflection of both who I am and who I pretend to be, as well as the possibility to see myself in an entirely new way if I was brave enough to take a leap of faith into the Great Unknown. But did I have the courage? Was I willing to see my reality for what it simply is – a hodgepodge of labels, concepts, ideas, attachments, and opinions, none of which were real and true? There was nothing I could do but observe the label-less, concept-less, idea-less, attachment-less reality that was opening up in front of me right here, right now, right in this moment, filling me with great wonder and surprise. In the here and now, nothing else existed but the opportunity to break free from all the trappings of the mind and taste something of the infinite. But will I bite?

"Keep asking, 'Who is in?'" Avikal instructed as he walked away.

Of all the times he had instructed us with this enigmatic Koan, of all the times I had received the Koan, taken the Koan in, held it, put my energy into it, opened myself up to it, dreamt of it, talked of it, put great effort into answering it; of all the times I racked my brain trying to figure out "who is in" like a complicated trigonometry problem, I suddenly got it, it clicked – not because I understood it, not because I gave up trying to understand it, but because I realized there was nothing to understand. Suddenly, all my efforts seemed futile, meaningless, counterproductive because it didn't matter! There was no answer to the question "who is in" because the question itself was futile! There was nothing to analyze, judge, or solve; nothing to want or wish for; no "shoulding", imagining, believing, guessing. What's the point in trying to find an answer to "who is in" if all my descriptions and interpretations were based on a deceptive, limited appearance of reality? In this Truth, reality was absolutely boundless, unlimited by time and space which meant the possibilities to experience myself were endless! What joy! What flight! What freedom! What... fear.

Fear. There it was. Staring right at me, teasing me, triggering me, showing me my attachment to my habits, my delusions, my pain, my person, my story. And there I was, sitting on a meditation cushion, doing nothing and facing everything. I knew that beyond this fear was the greatest mystery of my life: the mystery of my me-ness that was opening, expanding, waiting to be discovered. All I had to do was jump. Why is it so fucking scary to jump into your inner being? "To be yourself is the most difficult and simple thing you can do," I had scribbled Avikal's words in my notebook on Day 4 of the training. Why is it so terrifying to be yourself? In that moment, I gathered all the energy and vitality that was available to me and made the decisive choice to push past the fear. I had come so far in "ascending the Silver Mountain" which is how Avikal describes the poetry of enlightenment:

I am spending days with you beloveds,
Ascending the silver mountain.
I am here. We are together and yet,
you'll reach alone.
An ocean of truth surrounds the peak.

There was no turning back now. I braced myself and jumped into the ocean.

Who is in? – (The Jump)

It took years before I could find the words to describe my experience of *satori*. Perhaps the closest description is a line I heard almost a year later from the biopic film, *Ford v Ferrari*, in which Matt Damon plays the role of American race car driver Carroll Shelby. In the quote that bookends the film, we are in the "cockpit" of the car with Shelby as he races along a winding track, breaking a then-record speed of a racecar at 7,000 RPM. When I heard this line, it brought back the heart-pounding, euphoric, renewed, empowered, unstoppable, awe-inspired, exhilarated I'M-ON-TOP-OF-THE-FUCKING-WORLD sensations in my body that I briefly experienced in *satori*:

"There's a point – 7,000 RPM – where everything fades. The machine becomes weightless, it just disappears. And all that's left is a body moving through space and time. 7,000 RPM – that's where you meet it. You feel it coming – it creeps up on you close in your ear. Asks you a question; the only question that matters. Who are you?"

"Me," I said in a commanding voice that came out of me with a thrust of energy, causing my torso to bolt upright like one thunderstruck. My partner's eyes widened.

"Whoa!" I exclaimed. "That was weird! Something just happened." My heart was pounding. I sat even taller. I didn't know what that "something" was but the best word I can use to describe it is alignment. Pure alignment. As if all the components of my Being – body, heart, mind, soul – were parallel and perfectly in line with something else. But the question is with what?

"I'm gonna try it again," I said excitedly, with a childlike fascination akin to a baby recognizing its own reflection in the mirror for the first time. The listener is encouraged not to give any verbal cues to the speaker during Who Is In, but the corners of my partner's lips had turned upward, her blue eyes twinkling at me with glee. She was there, witnessing me teeter in the space Osho often talked about in his discourses – the space between awareness and madness, madness and awareness. Who knew there was such a fine line between the two? Moreover, who knew it would take so much courage to cross it?

"Me," I said again with even more gusto, more intensity, my torso leaning slightly forwards now, as if adjusting the coordinates of my body along a three-dimensional plane that would attune me to the Quantum. "Holy shit!" I shouted. It happened again. The something. The pure alignment. A click. This time, my partner's eyes were beaming with pleasure. She was smiling. "Go on," she beckoned with her eyes.

The next few minutes felt like hours, days, months, perhaps even years. My concept of time became confused; the seconds had slowed down yet everything seemed to be happening so fast. I continued repeating "me" over and over again, seizing the opportunity at every turn to make a statement about who I am with courage and commitment, intention and vitality. Avikal called it being in a "yes" place, a conscious choice we make when we surrender the ego and meet the moment with wonder, openness, and feminine receptivity. There's no effort, only a relaxed attitude towards what is. There's no goal, only surprise at what we find. There's no conflict, only curiosity. No seeking, only finding. Suchness.

"Me" became my personal mantra that carried me into that "yes" place, bringing me closer and closer to the deepest, most intimate parts of myself. There was a beautiful melody there, the music of my heart rang true and I wanted to stay and hear it but there were obstacles that kept getting in the way. Obstacles such as fear, uncertainty, doubt. Obstacles such as resistance, judgment, denial. Obstacles such as the past, present, and future. Yes, even the present became an obstacle because I was still watching it, still experiencing myself having an experience, still communicating my experience of each moment to my partner in words that sounded more like fragmented sound bites than complete sentences. It felt funny to speak, as if language itself was a contradiction, a combination of sounds that filled the gaps between two worlds, robbing the spirit of each moment like a still photograph. This contradiction was starting to nag at me; what would it take for me to experience reality directly, with no filter, no screen, no outside influence, no mind? Each moment required renewed intention, commitment, and courage. Each moment felt like a mini death and rebirth. Death and rebirth. Rebirth and death. Who knew there was such a fine line between the two?

At some point I knew I had to just let go – let go of myself, let go of the watcher, let go of the mental fucking clutter and just go for it. That point was here and now; it was now or never. It was a point that I had spent my whole teenage and young adult life searching for. The point of the eternal, the point that embodied something of the Real. The point at which time and space collapsed and there was only a formless existence that contained all the answers, all the mysteries, all the contradictions and paradoxes of life and all at once. The point at which all the points cancelled each other out and became point-less, amounting to nothing-ness – the center of the universe; the epitome of human existence that all the great mystics, masters, and sages talked about. Drugs, sex, and rock and roll had only given me a temporary glimpse into this experience at best, and a romanticized illusion of it at worse. The closest I had come to this point was through meditation, but even that had fallen short at times.

What would you do to hear the melody of your heart? Would you give up your ideas about good or bad, right or wrong, if only for a moment? Would you unfreeze your personality, if only briefly? Would you be willing to see your biggest fears as nothing more than everyday annoyances, if only slightly? Would you expand your capacity to treat your doubts and insecurities as mere background noise, if only a little? Would you give yourself permission to fully own up to the totality of who you are, if only reluctantly? Would you close your eyes and fall backwards into the gaping abyss, trusting that the universe will catch you? If only…

How to describe the experience of fully letting go? Uncertainty. Exhilaration. Freedom. Beauty. Bliss. There came a point where I no longer could describe it to my partner. There was nothing to describe – only everything to experience. But the watcher held on and continued watching. So I found myself caught between the folds of a multidimensional quantum field, dashing back and forth between watching my experience and disappearing into it. Watching and disappearing. Watching and disappearing. Disappearing and watching. The closer I got to myself, the more I disappeared into these folds. Worlds colliding. Identities collapsing. Hierarchies crumbling. Mysteries unfolding. Soon, there were no boundaries. I found myself in a paradox. A conundrum that contained all the polarities of life, both and neither at the same time. Both inside and outside. Both solid and liquid. Both mundane and sacred, earthly and unearthly, ordinary and extraordinary, existing completely and completely nonexisting. And for a moment, as brief and fleeting as it was, I, the subject, the one experiencing the experience, also ceased to exist. And all that was left was the melody.

The sweetest melody there ever was. A joyful melancholy of my heart's deepest longing to be seen and loved for who I am. My whole body vibrated and tingled with orgasmic aliveness. My genitals and face caught on fire. A great feeling of relief and exhilaration swept over me, the feeling of having lost something precious only to find it years later and in the most obvious location. To think that it was already there, it had always been there – always and already – Avikal's ode to Truth.

I leapt to my feet. I exploded into ecstasy. I thrashed my body around. I hoot and hollered. I howled. I squealed. I laughed. But it wasn't just any laughter; it came from a very deep, satisfying place in my inner belly and possessed every cell of my body. No control. Hysterical. Screaming. Couldn't stop. I was not laughing at that point. I *was* laughter. What was I laughing about? The absurdity of it all. Life. How seriously I take myself and how ridiculous it was to take myself so seriously. All the rituals I had created around my self-deception, self-absorption, self-pity, self-importance; how much time and energy I invested in reinforcing these rituals. How ridiculous and childish and foolish it all was. I kicked my feet around and danced like a woman gone mad upon these realizations. I was no longer afraid. There were thirty other people in the room, but I didn't care. I was alone. I didn't need anyone or anything. I was seen. I was loved. I was free.

After laughter, came the tears. Crying felt like a holy experience, an outpouring of emotion, an overflow of the heart, a prayer. My tears had a quality of ecstasy and pain in them. I took a long walk along the riverbank and listened to the silent serenading of Mother Nature, which reached and touched a place deep inside my heart. How could I have not heard it before? My heart felt tender and fragile, as if at any moment it could burst and shatter, as if the breeze, as gentle and friendly as it was, would push my heart past its breaking point. How could I not have felt it before? My eyes felt naked and raw; sensitive to light, as if seeing for the first time. The colors were rich, vibrant. How could I not have seen it before? My skin felt clean and soft, like a newborn baby. I sipped the air and walked through it slowly, mindfully, as if not to disturb the particles, as if not to take more than what I need. I felt undeserving of all the abundance that graced my sight to behold. Completely and utterly undeserving. I felt contrite for having taken so much of it for granted. I trembled with gratitude. There was nothing else I could do but fall to my hands and knees and surrender. I kissed the earth, asking for forgiveness, begging for mercy, promising the world for another chance.

My heart shattered into a million pieces; my tears poured through the fragments of shard and glass, tumbling down my face like little jewels. I was reminded of being a small child, how my mother – in her creative attempt to assuage my tantrums – would "collect" my tears from my eyelashes and cheeks and "stash" them away in the top shelf of our closet furthest from my reach, where she promised they turned into pearls, just like my birth name "Margarit" which means pearl in Armenian. On days when she was out, I would stand on a chair on my tiptoes and look for the pearls, only to feel disappointed not to find them. I always wondered about those pearls until I eventually grew up and forgot about them. Now I remembered. I had found them. I couldn't believe I had finally found them after all these years. And to think they were with me all along.

I knew that a profound transformation had occurred, and I would never be the same again. What I didn't know was how long it would take my conscious mind to understand, interpret, and integrate it with reality. As it would turn out, it took much longer than I expected. As it would also turn out, I was gravely mistaken to think I could be pure, and wise, and free all at once.

"What do I do with this information?" I asked Avikal days later.

"Celebrate and share."

Pramod Drazen Sivak
Actor and Director, Zagreb, Croatia

The first time, about 25 years ago, that I went to a Koan-based retreat, I felt as if I was on the wildest of rides. Since then the experience has changed forms, however, the essence is the same: naked and alone, facing one moment after another. And still, although I started the ride full of doubt and fear, I did not hesitate; a paradox.

All that I longed for, without consciously knowing it, was there – no scriptures, no gurus. The only tradition being that of individuals longing to wake up, reaching back as far as humanity does. It is a strange feeling, meeting something for the first time and feeling like it is familiar, as there is something utterly natural in practicing self-inquiry. It is not like learning a new language or a new skill, it is more like returning home. The approach is something intrinsic to humans; it seems it is only a matter of nurturing it.

Another paradox I met is that although self-inquiry felt like coming home, the route seemed to take me into unknown territory. The unknown meant "being outside" of ideas, concepts and experiences from the past and other people's knowledge. It meant finding the reverse of the mechanical and predictable in my behavior, relearning; experiencing one moment to another, and yet, standing firmly on the ground.

A strange thing I realized is that what I might find in that unknown territory could not come with me; so no pockets were needed. If I liked what I found and wanted to keep it for later, trying to hoard or prepare myself for the future, it would melt away like an ice cream in the summer sun. And if there was something I found I did not like at all and wanted to get rid of, thinking that it is not mine, or trying to save myself from the uncomfortableness, it would get more intense. So, I found that getting familiar with walking in the unknown was getting familiar with having my house more and more empty. And yet, the more my house emptied, the fuller it felt. Desires, knowledge, dreams, hankering for meaning, all fading and getting washed away, leaving – nothing. And what a nothing it is!

The aliveness and freshness need no doing, the only tool being the Koan itself. As it couldn't be preserved or put on a pedestal, it removes any crutch I might reach for, leaving me to fall flat on my face. It carries no "I told you so", keeping my feet firmly on the ground so that I can let go and find the unexpected or the unimaginable.

We live relying on a set of ideas that were handed on to us with the best of intentions, however, we rarely check them in reality. Is it true that I am my biography, my preferences, my education, my experiences of the past? That I am the sum of all that? It sounds like quite a setup. So, how can one continue without the handed-down idea of good and bad? With the ideas of good and bad one cannot but repeat, going on in circles with the pre-made patterns in dealing with the present moment. Self-inquiry peels those ideas, one by one, and the Koan is the knife.

Facing the moment without those ideas of good and bad, suddenly everything tips. Earth and heaven change places and the same old things don't look the same anymore. This shift makes my system rewire automatically, without my interference; finding myself laughing in the midst of personal drama or touched to the core by the ordinary. The usual tactics don't apply anymore, the usual perspective is worth nothing, and I have no choice but to keep the past out of the present moment.

The Koan does not preach. It is not a part of a moral code, not part of the spiritual and non-spiritual, it does not give moral guidance. So, the game we played with authority is gone. There is no one and nothing higher, nothing that allows us to play the victim of circumstances. It does not allow us to misuse it to overpower others or enable us to build dead monuments to show to others. It gives us tremendous responsibility, putting us in the center of the action, starting this moment, with no reference to the past. That allows us to join the real creation, breaking the vicious circle of blaming and not showing ourselves.

The freedom that comes out from this is not given by something or someone, and it is not a freedom one would easily accept. It asks for a commitment to keeping our eyes wide open. It does not wrap us up and comfort us in a pleasant and cozy safety; it straightens our spine and keeps us awake. With no past to rely on and no authorities and knowledge to refer to, we arrive at aloneness. This aloneness is, a new experience; not a lack of something, an absence, but an experience of being in the full company of ourselves. This immense liberation I felt by not leaning on others is like an explosion of possibilities. And it doesn't feel selfish or self-centered, just the opposite: I started seeing myself in others, in things and people I could not relate to before. There was a feeling of immediate connection, a warmth and joy of participating along with others.

The Koan does not make promises. It may look like a distant mountain, which does not lure us with hope of lush greenery and beautiful views. Very far away from the usual promise-giving that rushes that familiar drug of hope through our veins. It seems strange that the system addicted to living with a goal has not realized that this strategy has always unmistakably failed, that things never happened as was expected, and that there is a deep pain of being disappointed and let down. It immediately creates another goal. This part of our mind that wants to protect us is quick in adapting, so if the goal was material it can just adapt itself to the new environment and make a goal spiritual, again pushing our energy into fruitless action. The Koan brings things to the beginning, again and again, enabling us to slow down and quit running after a mirage, an image of a salvation moment that will finally send us on eternal holidays.

Any seriousness that might want to hide in there will not survive for long. The Koan cuts through illusion mercilessly, demanding: Now. Now. Now. The rigid small mind trying to take discoveries and make a new set of rules is just not able to survive the aliveness of the moment. Fresh air coming in and out does not allow stale and dead things around. It does not care in which aspect of our lives it resides: the way we eat, sleep, make love, relate to others, work or do nothing.

And then, the Koan is gone. There is no Koan, there is no self-inquiry, only us, dying and being born again, moment after moment. In those moments of clarity, I felt ridiculous. After a long and exhausting struggle, finding myself in the simplest of moments and without anything to show, I am literally not able to stop laughing loudly at myself. How can one shout about being thirsty while being immersed in water? Well, it takes some impressive skill to be so deluded and do just that. And still, though energy may seem to be wasted, it is not that I am left without it, quite the contrary. All that capacity to engage my energy in protecting myself from life (protect oneself from life? how is that even possible?) now turns into discovering and developing qualities that shift the perspective from surviving to living; a major shift.

It is not by accident the term "being reborn" is often used throughout the history of human consciousness. This shift into reality is such a turn I feel it work backwards and forwards, influencing my experiences in the past and affecting future steps, too.

In the beginning, I was surprised that I sometimes cried reading very simple lines from people from long ago, who were on the awakening path, saying things about their everyday life. I thought, "My God, I feel so touched as if it is my life." I realized there is no time or space that separates us in reality. It is only now. Now. Now.

In a very real sense, we are all aliens on a strange planet. We spend most of our lives reaching out and trying to communicate. If during our whole lifetime, we could reach out and really communicate with just two people, we are indeed very fortunate.
Gene Roddenberry, author

About the Author

Avikal is a mystic. Curiosity, passion and love for the truth guide his teaching and are transmitted in a clear and focused way. He is the founder and director of the Integral Being Institute active in Europe, Asia and Australia.

Avikal worked as an anthropologist and a freelance photographer.

His love for Martial Arts, which he began practicing in 1970, took him to teaching Aikido and Sword in 1987, while his love for the body produced diplomas and professional activity in Shiatsu, Yu-Ki and Seitai (healing techniques). From 1989 to 1994 he was the director of the Osho School for Centering and Zen Martial Arts, a faculty of the Multiversity in the ashram of the Indian mystic Osho in Pune, India.

He was Osho's photographer.

Being involved with Zen and Advaita for more than 35 years, he now leads retreats such as Satori and The Awareness Intensive. Since 1997 he has developed an innovative and original approach to the work with the Inner Judge and he is a well-known teacher of The Dimensions of Being (Essence) and the Enneagram.

He has also been working as a Life Coach, Management Trainer and Executives Mentor on presence, leadership, resilience and conflict resolution in Europe and Australia.

He is the author of: *When the Ocean Dissolves into the Drop*, LSWR 2016; *Freedom to Be Yourself: Mastering the Inner Judge*, O-Books, Winchester, UK/Washington, USA 2012; and *Without a Mask: Discovering Your Authentic Self*, O-Books, Winchester, UK/ Washington, USA 2011; and many more books in Italian.

Avikal is also a poet.

Other Titles by this Author

When the Ocean Dissolves into the Drop: Osho, Love, Truth and me

There is a point beyond which physics cannot venture: the event horizon, a region of space-time where phenomena cannot be registered. The event horizon is a bodiless border on the edge of a black hole; anything that the black hole's gravitational field attracts beyond this border will be unable to come back. All possibility of exploration stops here: no unfortunate astronaut who free-fell into the black hole could ever return. We do not know what lies in the black hole, beyond the event horizon. Science has never reached the other side. But spiritual seekers who make a leap beyond – yes, they know. And that is the subject of this book: the possibility of exploring beyond an imaginary confine, a journey of awareness in which one can enter, register phenomena, evaluate their implications, and reemerge with one's results. There is still a point of no return, but it is of a different kind: it is a threshold beyond which you can never be as you were, and from which you can never turn back. You cannot put your awakened self to death. Sri Ramana Maharshi explains this well: if the bucket (the ego) dips into the well (the self), but the cord is not severed, the ego can return, even after years of absence. In sahaja, though, one's natural state, this cord is finally severed and the ego cannot return. Here, in this book, Avikal takes us down into that well and shows us how to go about severing that rope.

From the introduction by Ma Prem Kiya/Ida Panicelli
Edizioni LSWR, Milan 2016

Freedom to Be Yourself: Mastering the Inner Judge

Inner judge, superego, barking dog are some of the different names for that presence that judges and evaluates every aspect of our inner and outer experience. The judgment is so fundamental to the way we function that we not only take it for granted, but accept it even when it is the cause of great suffering, misunderstanding and conflict. Many traditions take this presence to be one of the greatest obstacles on the spiritual path and in the endeavor of personal realization.

In *Freedom to Be Yourself*, Avikal E. Costantino uses his more than thirty years' experience of psychological and spiritual seeking to unravel the way this judge works and to show how it limits personal growth, sexuality, affective and work relationships, as well as any original expression of our potential. He provides exercises and inquiry to recognize the presence of the judge in daily life, and to begin the concrete transformation in our capacity of loving, creativity and individuality.

O-Books, Winchester, UK/Washington, USA 2012

Without a Mask: Discovering Your Authentic Self

Who is behind the mask that we have learnt to wear in order to survive and function in the world? Who are we really, behind familial and social conditioning? Is it possible to be spontaneous and authentic, or is it just an infantile desire to leave behind along with our dreams? This book tackles these themes and offers understanding and techniques for recognizing our authentic Self, helping us to realize that behind the personality mask there is a mysterious universe, an ocean of potentiality, and that is our true nature. When we begin to fully understand, the command "know yourself" will no longer just be the preserve of philosophers and mystics but will offer us the opportunity to ask the right questions, those that enable us to lift the veil that hides our true face and find peace and fulfilment.

O-Books, Winchester, UK/Washington, USA 2011

Lust, Love and Prayer – Lussuria, Amore e Preghiera

These poems are an overflowing of the heart and fire in the

genitals.

These poems are letting go, vulnerability, dissolution of boundaries.

Self-published.

The text is both in English and Italian.

www.integralbeing.com

O-BOOKS

SPIRITUALITY

O is a symbol of the world, of oneness and unity; this eye represents knowledge and insight. We publish titles on general spirituality and living a spiritual life. We aim to inform and help you on your own journey in this life.
If you have enjoyed this book, why not tell other readers by posting a review on your preferred book site?

Recent bestsellers from O-Books are:

Heart of Tantric Sex
Diana Richardson
Revealing Eastern secrets of deep love and intimacy to Western couples.
Paperback: 978-1-90381-637-0 ebook: 978-1-84694-637-0

Crystal Prescriptions
The A-Z guide to over 1,200 symptoms and their healing crystals
Judy Hall
The first in the popular series of eight books, this handy little guide is packed as tight as a pill-bottle with crystal remedies for ailments.
Paperback: 978-1-90504-740-6 ebook: 978-1-84694-629-5

Take Me To Truth
Undoing the Ego
Nouk Sanchez, Tomas Vieira
The best-selling step-by-step book on shedding the Ego, using the
teachings of *A Course In Miracles*.
Paperback: 978-1-84694-050-7 ebook: 978-1-84694-654-7

The 7 Myths about Love...Actually!
The Journey from your HEAD to the HEART of your SOUL
Mike George
Smashes all the myths about LOVE.
Paperback: 978-1-84694-288-4 ebook: 978-1-84694-682-0

The Holy Spirit's Interpretation of the New Testament
A Course in Understanding and Acceptance
Regina Dawn Akers
Following on from the strength of *A Course In Miracles*, NTI
teaches us how to experience the love and oneness of God.
Paperback: 978-1-84694-085-9 ebook: 978-1-78099-083-5

The Message of A Course In Miracles
A translation of the Text in plain language
Elizabeth A. Cronkhite
A translation of *A Course in Miracles* into plain, everyday
language for anyone seeking inner peace. The companion
volume, *Practicing A Course In Miracles*, offers practical lessons
and mentoring.
Paperback: 978-1-84694-319-5 ebook: 978-1-84694-642-4

Your Simple Path
Find Happiness in every step
Ian Tucker
A guide to helping us reconnect with what is really important in our lives.
Paperback: 978-1-78279-349-6 ebook: 978-1-78279-348-9

365 Days of Wisdom
Daily Messages To Inspire You Through The Year
Dadi Janki
Daily messages which cool the mind, warm the heart and guide you along your journey.
Paperback: 978-1-84694-863-3 ebook: 978-1-84694-864-0

Body of Wisdom
Women's Spiritual Power and How it Serves
Hilary Hart
Bringing together the dreams and experiences of women across the world with today's most visionary spiritual teachers.
Paperback: 978-1-78099-696-7 ebook: 978-1-78099-695-0

Dying to Be Free
From Enforced Secrecy to Near Death to True Transformation
Hannah Robinson
After an unexpected accident and near-death experience, Hannah Robinson found herself radically transforming her life, while a remarkable new insight altered her relationship with her father, a practising Catholic priest.
Paperback: 978-1-78535-254-6 ebook: 978-1-78535-255-3

The Ecology of the Soul
A Manual of Peace, Power and Personal Growth for Real People
in the Real World
Aidan Walker
Balance your own inner Ecology of the Soul to regain your
natural state of peace, power and wellbeing.
Paperback: 978-1-78279-850-7 ebook: 978-1-78279-849-1

Not I, Not other than I
The Life and Teachings of Russel Williams
Steve Taylor, Russel Williams
The miraculous life and inspiring teachings of one of the World's
greatest living Sages.
Paperback: 978-1-78279-729-6 ebook: 978-1-78279-728-9

On the Other Side of Love
A woman's unconventional journey towards wisdom
Muriel Maufroy
When life has lost all meaning, what do you do?
Paperback: 978-1-78535-281-2 ebook: 978-1-78535-282-9

Practicing A Course In Miracles
A translation of the Workbook in plain language, with
mentor's notes
Elizabeth A. Cronkhite
The practical second and third volumes of The Plain-Language
A Course In Miracles.
Paperback: 978-1-84694-403-1 ebook: 978-1-78099-072-9

Quantum Bliss
The Quantum Mechanics of Happiness, Abundance, and Health
George S. Mentz
Quantum Bliss is the breakthrough summary of success and
spirituality secrets that customers have been waiting for.
Paperback: 978-1-78535-203-4 ebook: 978-1-78535-204-1

The Upside Down Mountain
Mags MacKean
A must-read for anyone weary of chasing success and happiness
– one woman's inspirational journey swapping the uphill slog for
the downhill slope.
Paperback: 978-1-78535-171-6 ebook: 978-1-78535-172-3

Your Personal Tuning Fork
The Endocrine System
Deborah Bates
Discover your body's health secret, the endocrine system, and
'twang' your way to sustainable health!
Paperback: 978-1-84694-503-8 ebook: 978-1-78099-697-4

Readers of ebooks can buy or view any of these bestsellers by
clicking on the live link in the title. Most titles are published
in paperback and as an ebook. Paperbacks are available in
traditional bookshops. Both print and ebook formats are
available online.
Find more titles and sign up to our readers' newsletter at
http://www.johnhuntpublishing.com/mind-body-spirit
Follow us on Facebook at https://www.facebook.com/OBooks/
and Twitter at https://twitter.com/obooks